ANOTHER SEASON IN ASTON

Dave Woodhall

First published in Great Britain in 2009 by
Heroes Publishing.
P.O. Box 1703, Perry Barr,
Birmingham B42 1UZ.

ISBN: 978-0-9559708-2-5

Cover photo: Steve Beauchampe

Printed by Thomson Litho

Contents

Introduction

Those whom the Gods wish to destroy they first make mad.

They'd do the job a lot easier if they made the intended Those who support the Villa for a bit. The end result of 2008-09 happens regularly and we should be used to it by now. Get so far, build our hopes up, have us think this time it really will be different, then knock us back to earth with a series of accidents, calamities and downright daft decisions that combine to make us wonder why we bothered in the first place. It was always going to end in tears and bigger fool you if you thought different.

If that sounds cynical, sorry. I didn't always think that way, but decades of watching the Villa has given me a highly-developed sense of belief that success will inevitably be followed by crashing disappointment. For every European Cup there's bound to be subsequent relegation. Ron Saunders will eventually be succeeded by Billy McNeill. Brian Little's shirt will one day be worn by Warren Aspinall. You may as well get used to it – it's bound to happen. Maybe we prefer it that way; success gets boring after a while and in any case we wouldn't know what to do with it. We're Brummies. We enjoy moaning.

Watching the Villa in 2008-09 wasn't that bad. In fact, most of it was enjoyable. There were some memorable matches, great results, a record-breaking string of away wins and, biggest surprise of the lot, the rare sight of the wider football world taking note of what was going on at Villa Park and approving of it. There were also annoying defeats, disappointing performances and the first unpopular decision made by Martin O'Neill in almost three years. Build 'em up, knock 'em down. We should be used to it by now.

It all added up to yet another season in Aston watching the most beautifully-named football team in the world (© T. Hanks). Read on and enjoy.

Pre-season

And the fun begins

13th June: Nobody quite knows these days where one season ends and the next kicks off again, but the announcement that Villa are donating their shirt sponsorship deal to children's hospice Acorns gets the anticipation off to a good start. It's an astonishing idea and one which will get the club a multitude of good publicity over the coming season. Mac's invited to the kit launch and is most perturbed to find there's no freebies, either food, drink, shirts or women.

15th June: Liverpool make their opening bid for Gareth Barry, who couldn't make his desire to sign for them more obvious. Well, he could make a proper transfer request but it would cost him money and he doesn't want a move THAT desperately.

27th June: I'm flicking through the papers in the WH Smith library when this little gem jumps out of an interview with former Villa manager (yes, it still sounds good) David O'Leary. "*There are still Villa fans who thank me for what I did there.*" Let's see... average gate just over forty thousand. That would make maybe half a dozen who think the earth is flat. That'll be them, then.

2nd July: "*Why do Birmingham City exist?*" is a question that's puzzled philosophers down the ages. H&V solicitor Dennis Dudley reckons the reason for their being is so that they don't have to be invented. But don't expect any sense tfrom the legal profession. I reckon it's to give fanzine editors something to fill blank pages. Over the years the publication I'm loosely associated with has had many a happy hour reporting the goings on at the Bordesley Green Palace of Varieties, and today comes another. David Sullivan, a self-made man and it's good of him to take the blame, is helping the police with their enquiries once more. This time it's to do with a 25-year-old woman at his Essex mansion. I know potential sex crimes are no laughing matter but there's always something unsavoury wherever David Sullivan might be.

9th July: After a few weeks of moaning that we haven't signed anyone there's a report that Villa are interested in Chelsea's Steve Sidwell. He's okay I suppose, but nothing special. Anyway, he was happy to jump from Reading to Chelsea's bench on a free so money's obviously his main motivator.

10th July: I've been wrong about players before and Steve Sidwell is one of them. On reflection he's a hardworking midfielder and he'll do well for us if Barry leaves. It's just as well we've signed him today then, for around £5.5 million although the exact figure is, of course 'undisclosed'. What's the point of this new addition to the football vocabulary? Probably something to do with tax avoidance, and almost certainly in the interests of making players a few bob better off. Taking of tax avoidance, the first team are on a tour of Switzerland and tonight is their first game. **FC Wii 0 Villa 6**, with a team consisting of first teamers, squad players and young hopefuls.

12th July: It's a good job pre-season results don't really matter as we go down to a 1-2 defeat against FC Zurich, Sidwell making his debut.

15th July: Lincoln City are memorable for two things. They're where Sir Graham Taylor started his managerial career and there used to be a fine run of pubs along one side of the High Street between the station and the ground. I don't know if they're all still there or how many of them were used by the players tonight but there has to be an excuse for **Lincoln City 3 Villa 1**. After going a goal up within five minutes we were crap and our supporters gave a lengthy and pointless rendition of that song about never winning the European Cup. This report originated from Dave Bridgwater, who's daft/fanatical enough to go to Lincoln midweek for a friendly. I was minding my own business at home, sticking on the radio to find out the score and suddenly it was Groundhog Day. "*Police are to interview Birmingham City chairman David Sullivan....*" They're only a fortnight out of date I thought, and was about to send a strongly-worded letter to the Director-General of the BBC when I listened a bit more and found out that this was a different set of Peelers and a different investigation. This time it's corruption, again.

19th July: Odense (away). There was a time when a trip like this would have had me perusing first the Teletext cheap flights pages and later on the internet for the best deals. Now I remember some time during mid-afternoon that Vila are playing a European tie and switch the radio on to find out we've drawn 2-2, with John Carew and Martin Laursen scoring for us. Steve Sidwell got an unfortunate own goal and we let in a soft injury-time equaliser. I hope that's not an omen.

22nd July: Walsall (away). One of football's finer traditions is the annual pre-season friendly at Bescot. Not only is it a pleasant evening out renewing old acquaintances, but I write a piece for the programme and in return get a few tickets for the main stand. In the past I've found myself sitting next to Des Bremner and Gordon Cowans but tonight I have to make do with the company of the press pack, starring David O'Leary's mate Bill Howell in a very bad pair of shorts.

The crowd for this game has dropped every season, as both sets of supporters realised Villa field what's usually little more than a reserve team, although there were a few more going along tonight out of curiosity as Gareth Barry is down to play. He got a strange reaction, plenty of booing at the start together with some very exaggerated clapping from a few supporters, who seemed to grow in numbers as the game wore on. The mischief-maker in me wonders if we're going to have the first recorded sight of Villa supporters fighting amongst themselves at a pre-season but it's soon all peaceful. Whenever anything like this happens events always follow the same pattern. First it's the player's fault, then after a couple of days he gets defended and then, by the end of the week, the supporters who've had a go back at him are to blame for their 'disgusting' behaviour. It was the same when Savo spat at Blackburn, when Lee Hendrie had his rant at Bescot a couple of years ago and it'll happen now. Barry's substituted on the hour and it's noticeable that he and Martin don't look at each other. Both men leave well before the final whistle. If you're interested in the score, we were a goal down twice and won 3-2 in the end.

26th July: Odense (home). It seems weird to be playing a proper match at home in July, especially when Villa Park will shut up shop again for another three weeks before the season proper starts. Over 30,000 are here thanks to a mixture of decent prices and good weather. To go over an old theme it's not long ago we would have been glad of that crowd for the first league game of the season.

A lot of kids are around and it seems the good weather has encouraged a few older kids to have a drink or two more than they would usually. It'll catch up with you one day, chaps. New signing Brad Friedel, a snip at £2.5 million form Blackburn, is introduced to the crowd wearing a quite poor shirt. The money he's on, he could afford better.

There's a bit of an Aston Villa XI feel to the team. Stuart

Taylor's in goal with Craig Gardner at right-back and a Villa Park debut for Steve Sidwell. After the drama of the previous few days Gareth Barry's on the bench and receives a good reception during the warm-up. Unfortunately it's not long before he's back on the pitch. Wilfred Bouma goes into a tackle and instinctively you know it's a bad one. Maybe not Luc Nilis career-ending bad, but it's going to be a long time before Freddie plays again. Without a replacement left back I can think of it looks like Martin's going to have to be spending again sooner rather than later.

Barry is welcomed warmly onto the pitch, which given the circumstances was always likely, and played tidily enough without ever breaking sweat. Ashley Young scored a corking goal when he beat a couple of players and hit a 20 yard shot just after half-time. If he keeps that up he could be the first bit of genuine top-level class seen in our team since Paul McGrath left. We've had players who flattered to deceive, Juan Pablo Angel for one, and others such as Paul Merson who could turn it on against poor opposition but invariably went missing in the big games. Young, like Gabriel Agbonlahor, has that something about him to make you think he won't be fazed whatever the occasion.

John Carew hit the bar in the second half but nothing else of note happened as we closed the game out with no real drama and qualified for the UEFA Cup. Only 17 games stand between us and glory.

30th July: Liverpool have bought Robbie Keane for £20 million (yes, the same Robbie Keane we wouldn't pay another £500,000 for what seems an eternity ago) and are offering us £16.5 million for Barry. Villa say he's going nowhere now, because da Pool have missed some deadline we didn't tell them about.

1st August: Brad Guzan, who we wanted to sign last season but he couldn't get a work permit, finally moves from the American club Chivas. I ponder on why he's suddenly improved in the last six months but quickly realise that trying to get to the bottom of the FA's logic would take a lot longer than the time I've got left on this earth.

2nd August: Reading (away). It's a bit strange to have a friendly against a team you played in the league last season, but Reading's a decent ground with a good pitch and it's not too far away so it makes sense. Steve Sidwell's not playing, because yet again our biggest summer signing has got injured during training. Neither is Reading left-back Nicky Shorey, who was linked with a move to Villa Park within seconds of Freddie Bouma's injury. Brad Friedel makes an appearance, saving a penalty, and Curtis Davies gets a runout for the first hour and a bit. Gabby Agbonlahor scores a welcome second-half equaliser but the full team have got to do a bit better than this in a fortnight's time.

6th August: While no-one was looking Villa booked a short break in Spain and got a 1-1 draw with Linense from the third division. I don't know what the attendance was but I could probably name at least 90% of the away following.

7th August: It must be just a coincidence, but while Martin's out of the country we sign not one but two full-backs. Nicky Shorey is costing £4 million while Middlesbrough right-back Luke Young is ours for a million more. A half-hearted argument breaks out on the internet about why it's taken so long to get a right-back when we've needed one for two years but now is not the time for dissent.

8th August: Marbella (away). There's probably worse places to watch football than the south of Spain in August. Marbella are a second division side featuring Tommy Mooney, who was a promising youngster when he was with us, but his career never took off. He was with Watford for ages, had a few years at Small

Heath and a time at Walsall. Now he's winding his career down in Spain, which is pretty high up the 'nice work if you can get it' ladder. The last friendly sees the best performance with goals from Nathan Delfouneso, who's showing promise, and Craig Gardner, who's beginning a massive season. Wages have come on so much in the past decade that if he doesn't make it in the Premier League I don't think he'll have to end his days in the Spanish second division.

11th August: It seems like just another Monday morning, then Villa announce that we're 'in talks' with Rangers defender Carlos Cuellar. Scottish Player of the Year last season, and although that might not mean much he's an experienced player who always looks good on the very occasional times I glance at lower-level football on TV.

12th August: Deal wrapped up, Carlos Cuellar is now 'of Aston Villa'. He's a scruffy looking bugger though. The money he's on, he could surely afford to dress a bit better.

14th August: Hafnarfjordur (away). It's been 27 years since we last played in Iceland, the second leg of a European Cup tie against Valur Rekjavik. We went on to win the trophy so it's an omen that today we return to the country. I've always fancied Iceland – former Villa photographer/legend Terry Weir said it was the most memorable place he visited – but it's also ruinously expensive. That'll be a no then. Everyone who went over had a great time, with plenty of tasty geysers to spot and a surprisingly large amount of local Villa supporters in attendance. Slowly but surely we're taking over the world.

Gareth Barry's playing, which means he's ineligible for anyone else (ie Liverpool) in Europe this season and takes four minutes to put us a goal up. It was made by Ashley Young, who scored another two minutes later and was on top form throughout the game. Gabby Agbonlahor made it 3-0, although the home side pulled a goal back on half-time. Second half was a bit of a stroll, with Martin Laursen getting another and 4-1 will make the second leg a formality. In three days time the real thing starts and the opposition won't be straight off the trawlers.

August

The sun always shines on opening day

17th August: Manchester City (home). Here we go for the start of a brand new league season. There's always plenty of optimism around, even if more often than not it's misplaced. I can never forget putting money on us to win the league after a bright pre-season in 1986 and we all know what happened at the end of that one. It was the stupidest bet since Mrs Francis put ten bob on her little Lucifer to win the Bonniest Baby of 1954 contest.

It's the first time I've approached the ground from Witton Lane since last May and the new Tesco just past the island is open and visible. As Billy the badgeman says, when you've got a supermarket next to the ground you can rely on two things – clean toilets and vaguely healthy food. Fair point; it's surprising how often the surroundings of a football ground lack these two basic essentials.

The weather's good, trade's brisk and I get the chance to talk to Dave Wallace, editor of the City fanzine King of the Kippax. Dave's one of the best supporters you could wish to meet – when Frannie Lee was briefly chairman of City he was elected to be the fan representative on the board and got shot at repeatedly from all sides. Lee said Dave should be backing the board, some fans complained that he was pro-club, others said he was too critical of them, he was called a sell-out, a stooge and a professional complainer. In reality he was doing his best for supporters and those who condemned him for it were either too stupid to realise or jealous because they weren't good enough to do the job themselves.

A strange thing usually takes place whenever Manchester City travel to Villa Park. No sooner does their team coach swing through the gates and into the North Stand car park than the players it contains are transformed into Supermen. Clogging midfielders are reborn in the image of Michel Platini. Inept defenders are blessed with the spirit of McGrath. Strikers who wouldn't even recognise a cow's arse whether or not they were holding a banjo become goal machines. The end product is a team that has bounced from mid-table mediocrity down to the old third division and back again having the sort of record at Villa Park you'd expect if Milan joined the Premier League.

However, and this is bound to be tempting fate, City have got a chairman who's wanted back home in Thailand for fraud, they've just lost at home to an unpronounceable Danish team in the UEFA Cup and their only striker, Valeri Bojinov, gets injured in the warm-up. Surely they can't win today.

The match kicks off in front of a less-than-capacity crowd, which is one of the great quirks of life with Aston Villa. Our crowds always start off poorly and get better as the season progresses, no matter how we're doing. During a lull in the play I have a quick look around and it seems most of our neighbours have renewed. I'm glad about that – we haven't had any of the arsehole behaviour that made vacating the previous spec on the Holte necessary, and newcomers might not know the code of quiet contemplation that makes our corner of the North Stand so attractive. Ray Fairfax, former ticket office manager and before that Albion right-back, is just over the aisle from us. Ray's another of the good guys, who had to take a lot of flak because he worked at Villa Park when Doug's presence meant that to some people everything the club did was wrong. But that's all in the past, Ray still comes down the match and can give us the benefit of football through the eyes of someone who knows more about the game than any of us self-appointed experts could dream of.

We're up against the Micah Richards show in the first half as he holds out against everything we can throw at him. Richards was born in Birmingham, even if it was only because his parents were on holiday here at the time, and that means he's unquestionably a Villa fan. So why isn't he playing for us? It's not as though the city has been a hot-bed of footballing talent over the years. Craig Gardner and Gabby Agbonlahor at the moment. Darius Vassell, Tony Daley and Mark Walters in the past. Apologies if I've missed anyone out but for a city of a million people over a quarter of a century that's a pretty poor showing.

Two minutes after the break we get a goal only to fall asleep afterwards and our new full-backs Nicky Shorey and Luke Young combine well to provide City with a penalty from which they equalise. They look like they can go on to win, but Gabby shows his promise with a hat-trick inside seven minutes. It might or might not be A New Premier League Record as they say on the telly but I'm too busy jumping up and down to bother. You'd think they'd have a decent enough interval between goals, time to let you get your breath back. Three in seven minutes is just too quick; no sooner have I sat down than I have to leap up again. I'm not going overboard about Gabby, we've seen too many promising talents end up at Kidderminster, but we may as well enjoy it while it lasts.

City get a last-minute second goal, which allows us to complain that our defence still isn't right but the Barton's Arms post-mortem will be a happy one. Football's back.

22nd August: And so is Shaun Maloney, back to Celtic for £2.5 million. He was a decent player but his heart never seemed in it and a good profit on the deal makes it worthwhile.

23rd August: Stoke City (away). When Stoke got promoted there was all sorts of comment about how they'd be relegated by Christmas and their notorious fans would cause mayhem everywhere. I went along with the first but wasn't too sure about the second. They might have a bad reputation but the Premier League has a strange effect on clubs with bad reputations. Bolton used to be a right evil place to visit but it's a doddle now, while even Small Heath usually behave themselves on their fleeting visits to their betters. This is not a theory I intend to rely on should Millwall get promoted.

Some Stoke fans have been on a cyber charm offensive, visiting messageboards on goodwill missions. We'll have to see what they're like in 3-D but they'll doubtless be a handful for their opening home game. Losing at Bolton on the first day of the season mean that one bookie, with an eye for publicity, has already paid out on them getting relegated so they'll be even more up for it. Percy the world's most optimistic man thinks different. From the minute I pick him up near his palatial north Solihull apartment block he's full of enthusiasm about how Gabby and Ashley will carve open the plodding Stoke defence and carry on the goalscoring form of last Sunday. Much as I share his hope, I also remember he regards Paul Weller as the greatest songwriter of all time so Percy's opinions are not 100% reliable.

The Britannia's not a new ground for me – I went there with Dave Woodley when Brian Little was Stoke manager and for some reason we ended up on the pitch during a demonstration against their board. This is the first time I've driven there, though, and things have obviously changed. Once off the M6 there are signs to the ground and you can tell you're getting close when information boards sprout up along the road - "***WELCOME TO THE BRITANNIA STADIUM. DON'T EVEN THINK ABOUT PARKING HERE.***" "***OR HERE EITHER. HAVE A NICE DAY.***"

As I'm early I follow my own directions to a pub a mile or so away, which in Stoke means a different town. Parking up outside is like entering a time warp. Terraced houses, empty street corners, hardly any cars parked. The pub I've found is worth the detour and a pleasant pint or two is knocked back before the drive to the ground. Percy's a bit scared, as he is every time he encounters a life form that lives less than eight storeys high, but luckily there are a couple of Jam fans he can converse with. He starts by asking them what they think of Paul Weller's new work. They say they're not sure but it can't be as bad as the last couple of Style Council albums. I'd like to ask them if they realise he's been solo for twenty years, but think better of it.

Off to the ground and we manage to find the last space in what is euphemistically called a car park but is really a cul de sac on an industrial estate. I wonder if the man collecting the five pound notes has any connection with the companies based here or if he just brought a fluorescent jacket and a home-made sign along with him on the off-chance. We get to our seats just in time for kick-off and there's a right old atmosphere. Stoke are making a racket, that Delilah song is being pumped out and just for a moment I forget my air of supercilious cynicism and begin to enjoy myself. The mood soon passes.

As you'd imagine Stoke go for the throat from kick-off. After half an hour we have a stonewall penalty appeal turned down then Stoke straightaway attack and Rory Delap goes down under the weight of a challenge from Martin Laursen that wouldn't have felled Ronnie Corbett. If little teams are penalised by referees how do you explain this, eh? One-nil.

Half time sees the usual reunions between long-lost friends who haven't seen each other for at least three months as well as a lot of singing and boisterous behaviour including the now-obligatory throwing around of drinks. It's expensive enough without giving it away. The police and stewards are a tolerant bunch and the interval passes off without undue incident. We come out after the break looking more like a side that's going to compete with teams like Stoke. We score twice, thanks to Carew and Laursen, but in between Ricardo Fuller had given Stoke the lead again for a few minutes, with a goal straight out of the Route One Handbook. The crowd noise goes up a notch or three and just when we think a draw is a fair result Delap launches one of his trademark long throws which bounced off someone's head and into the net. When you equalise with six minutes left that should be enough for at least a point and it's not as though we hadn't been told about their not-so-secret weapon constantly since last season ended, but it was written in the stars that this was to be plucky little Stoke's day.

There's a bit of 'banter' between both sets of supporters as they leave the ground but most of the banterers shut up once they're within striking distance of each other. There are later reports that a Villa fan was attacked by a Stoke throwback, who was immediately handed over to the police by some of his own supporters. Well done to those concerned if this is the truth. As expected there's a lengthy queue of traffic back to the main road, but the police are keeping things moving better than they do at Villa Park and we're on the motorway with the minimum of fuss. As we head home Percy launches into an expert analysis, trying to convince me that losing your first away game to relegation favourites is a natural sign of progression.

It wasn't the hell-hole we'd been expecting but there's no doubt that Stoke's direct approach and the noise their supporters make will surprise more than just the Villa this season. Whether that will keep them up is another matter.

27th August: Now here's a development. James Milner, formerly at Villa on loan and since then a regular transfer target, has handed in a transfer request at Newcastle.

28th August: Hafnarfjordur (home). Few things in life are more pointless than the second leg of a cup tie when you're already three goals up. Talk before the game was of double figure scorelines, and even if that was out of the question we should be able to run up our highest aggregate in Europe (8-0, against Valur in 1981.) Someone on our website had a couple of tickets that were going free to good homes so I grabbed them for Percy and me. It's his birthday so I kindly gave one to him as a present. All heart, me.

The hard work was done a fortnight ago so it was no surprise that a few of the big names were rested. The team we did put out played fairly well at first, with Wayne Routledge impressive. 27 minutes gone and Marlon Harewood crossed for Craig Gardner to put us a goal up and it was looking good for that record victory. Then out of nowhere three minutes later Brad Friedel pushed out a shot into the path of an Icelander with an unpronounceable name ending in –sson and the scores were level.

Nothing much happened after that, with Villa content to pass the ball round and Hafnarfjordur battling away like their lives depended on it. Things fizzled out well before the final whistle (which was nowhere near as loud as the whistles every time their blonde physio came onto the pitch) and although there was a healthy 25,000 in the ground a load had left early, which made getting away from the traffic almost as easy as it was in the days of Graham Turner.

Haf...etc's team celebrated the draw as though they'd won the trophy, which in a way they had. Excuse the arrogance but we expect to be in the running to win the UEFA cup. Icelandic part-timers should never even dream of getting a draw at Villa Park.

29th August: £12 million is now the going price for an England under-21 midfielder. It's a lot of money but at least Milner won't have any problems adjusting to his new home. Then again, it's an entirely new club since he was last here so I hope he can cope with the change.

31st August: Liverpool (home). When we drew 0-0 with Liverpool two seasons ago someone came out of the Witton Lane stand almost apoplectic with rage. "*That was the worst bloody game I've ever seen.*" he spluttered at me, as though I was responsible. "*So?*" I replied. "*So you're supposed to write about it,*" he shouted back as he disappeared in the direction of Witton Island. I did write about it, but unfortunately it didn't make any difference. It had still been a crap goalless draw no matter how many times I wrote 'Villa 6 Liverpool 0'. Afterwards I was talking about the match in the Barton's when some elderly Liverpool supporter at the next table leaned over and started ranting in a Black Country accent about how football isn't that important and we shouldn't get upset about it. Obviously no friend of Mr Worst-Match-Ever but they had one thing in common. Why pick on me?

Liverpool is one of my three least favourite home games of the season (the others being Manchester United and Manchester United in the FA Cup) and the reason is clear when standing on Witton Lane for any length of time. Their out-of-town support might not be as big as United's, but it's not far behind. Si Page and I once counted the coaches leaving after one game against Liverpool (we're sad like that). 33 in total, 24 from Wales. We're almost as bad, with the number of Villa leisurewear-ing grown adults wanting to know which stand they're sitting in and where they can get a programme endangering the all-time record. Fair enough, we all went to our first match once but when you're in your thirties and live in Walsall you should be ashamed. What kept you?

Whenever there's a big game there's always the potential for problems in the North Stand as it's the prime target for away fans with tickets in our areas. Provided they keep their gobs shut and don't celebrate too loudly I don't have much of a problem with it, but some get very worked up although the ones shouting the most are usually out of harm's way. There's no goals today, so no subsequent meerkat impersonations. The internet warriors were doing their best to make Rafael Benitez's first trip here since the Gareth Barry transfer deal finally spluttered out into a Welcome To Hell expedition, but nobody seemed really bothered. There were a few songs, a bit of booing and a rather sad banner, but this is Villa Park. We save our raw emotion for those who deserve it.

James Milner comes on for his first Villa Park appearance and does alright. Because he's been here before and he played for

Leeds when he was in the juniors people think Milner's the finished article when he's still only 22. His fee will undoubtedly be a millstone at times but let's judge him for what he is, a promising youngster, rather than moan when he's not the final piece in our title-winning jigsaw.

In previous seasons we've either matched a poor Liverpool side or rolled over for them. Today they're definite title contenders but only played as well as we let them. That might not sound much of an improvement, but it was definitely there and we can take something from it.

September

Holidays already

15th September: Spurs (away). It's now compulsory that no sooner has the season got underway than everything stops so Ingerlund can play a friendly. A free Saturday for that and another one follows because we've had our first trip to dat dere Lundun shifted to also become our first Monday night match of the season.

If you've the inclination, the easiest way to get to Spurs is train from Liverpool Street to White Hart Lane. This gives you the opportunity, if it's midweek and they're therefore open, to try out some fine, if expensive, pubs in the City. When your visit coincides, as mine did today, with the announcement that thousands of bankers are to lose their jobs you can also laugh at the panic setting in amongst the yuppie scum who have poured scorn on us poor Northerners for years. White Hart Lane (the ground) might be set in an area of urban dereliction, but the approach to White Hart Lane (the station) is surprisingly pleasant, through London Fields and Hackney.

Spurs used to be one of the nastiest grounds in the league to visit. Standing in the away end, surrounded by thugs who would use their half-time trip to the toilet to choose their intended target and often they'd be able to get so close they'd inform you of the fact. The walk down to Seven Sisters tube in 1985 has become a thing of legend. Only a hundred or so of us endured it, but there were more who say they were there now than claim to have watched Oasis at the Jug of Ale. As time went by the threat of mutilation declined but the away terrace was still crap; it was reckoned that the best view was looking at the TVs in the West Stand executive boxes. But that was then, and this is now. The hooligans of old are still at the tube but now they're looking for tourists rather than away fans and "*Got the time mate?*" has been replaced by "*Tickets?*"

Wandering towards the turnstiles I get stopped by an over-officious policeman who wants to know why I've got a large bag in the vicinity of a football ground. He's satisfied by the explanation. And then along comes a vacuous Setanta presenter and camera crew. One of my particular hates in modern football is TV companies expecting that because they've bought the game, supporters will do whatever they want them to in the way of stupidity for the cameras. I hate this almost as much as I hate the idiots who go out of their way to be stupid for the cameras.

Before the game I see my Spurs-supporting buddy Jeff, who might have the best job in history. He runs the 100 Club in Oxford Street, one of the most famous music venues in the world. The 100 has resisted all attempts to gentrify it and is a bit of an embarrassment to Westminster Council, who would probably like to have it knocked down and a Hard Rock Cafe stuck on the site. Every time there's a story about how the club might be in danger Jeff gets a load of calls from the likes of Mick Jagger and the Gallagher brothers, offering to chain themselves to the bulldozers. I also see the same bloke I saw last season, who wants to collect tickets from every game in the league and walks round the queue asking if anyone just happens to have a stub from Stoke in their pocket.

Last season was the infamous 4-1 up and it finished 4-4 game, when Marlon Harewood won their man of the match award after doing everything in his power to cost us victory. This season Marlon's hopefully being kept out of harm's way back at home but no, he's on the bench again. If Spurs lose tonight it will be their worst start to a season for 34 years. They've got £22.5 million of debuts being made in the shape of Roman Pavlyuchenko and Vedran Corluka but their defence still gave us enough space for Nigel Reo Coker to score after five minutes.

There's plenty of "*Getting sacked in the morning*" -type songs, especially after a weak shot from Ashley Young creeps under the body of Gomes and just over the line in the 54th minute. There's going to be no repeat of last season, you can guarantee it. We're well on top and our first win in London for years is going to happen right here, right this minute. Then there's the unmistakable sight of Marlon Harewood getting ready to come on, and he replaces Milner with half an hour left. No, it can't happen again. No.

Five minutes to go and Bent scores for Spurs. Two thousand minds react with but a single thought. Fortunately lightning indeed doesn't strike twice and after at least an hour's stoppage time the whistle blows and we've picked up a useful three points. It'd be nice to think Spurs would get relegated, but in reality they've got too many decent players. They're a win or two off being a useful side even if they're going to have to wait a bit longer to get one.

I'd managed to get to the end of a row, so by the time the referee had finished blowing for full time I was out in the street and dashing towards the station. Not too long in a queue, on and away. Central, or whoever runs the trains out of Aston on matchdays, could learn a lot from TfL. Mussolini got the trains to run on time and Ken Livingstone sorted out London's public transport as well. Let's hope Boris Johnson can do the same. It's too much to ask that the Virgin home could be delayed for 15 minutes so I could get that one, but at least I made last orders in the Doric Arch just outside Euston. There's no better waiting room than a pub with good beer.

Midweek trains out of Euston are usually a lot quieter than on Saturdays and sleep is just about possible. I get a table with four seats all to myself, it leaves on time and at not long after 1.15 we're pulling into the International. Maybe Virgin, like the Villa, are finally getting their act together for the capital.

16th September: Lovers of quality radio rejoice, for Danny Baker's back on 606. It takes him less than a minute to have a dig at the Villa but that's allowed because it's from a proper supporter rather than a "*Who is Aston Villa?*" new fan.

18th September: Litex Lovich (away). They're from Bulgaria and in the absence of anyone who fancies picking me up in a private jet for the afternoon I'm at home trying to get a picture via the wonders of the internet. No sooner do I settle down to watch the match than it becomes apparent that we've already, scarcely a month into the season, got into a familiar pattern. Rest a few players for a cup match, let the opposition start well, go a goal down. Nigel Reo Coker equalised just before half-time and our two second-half goals matched Litex's two dismissals as the game turned a bit strange. Or maybe it was the streaming I was watching it on. The home leg should be a formality, but yet again none of the fringe players has given Martin a selection problem.

21st September: Albion (away). This used to be as big a deal as going to the Sty. How and why the rivalries have changed over the years is a matter of great sociological debate, but coming from over that way nothing's changed as far as I and every other Black Country-born Villa supporter I know, is concerned. It's the Albion and they're there to be hated, loathed and despised in equal measure.

They've got a drum, and a lot of noise. All little clubs having their season in the Premier League like to go on about how much noise they make but Albion take it one step further, they're contenders for the self-appointed crown of Best Supporters in the World, just like Newcastle, and we all know how nauseating that lot can be. Albion do it a bit differently though. As H&V contributor Alex Russon once said, they want it both ways. On one hand they want to make out that they're a friendly little club doing ever so well to be in the Premier League and there to enjoy themselves. Think Walsall drawn away to Manchester

United in the FA Cup and you'll be close. On the other they call us arrogant because we've widened our horizons beyond avoiding relegation.

An Albion player is injured in the warm-up – again – and we're underway. For a nice little club who don't want to make enemies they intend to shit on the Villa a lot. This confirms the First Rule of West Midlands Football, Subsection Two, namely that clubs intend to shit on the Villa in inverse proportion to how often they manage it. Albion tap the ball around as expected but don't look like scoring. On the other hand we get two goals in 90 seconds, courtesy of Messrs Carew and Agbonlahor. It looks like we could be on for another demolition derby, but Brad Friedel drops both a bollock and the ball, giving them the chance to pull a goal back.

Second half is much the same as the first. Albion get their supporters all excited by keeping the ball while we stand around looking unconcerned and hit the woodwork three times. The end of the match sees a group of Albion fans making rude gestures at us, which won't have done their image as the Green Party of the Premier League much good. We've got three points, which does our image as top four contenders a lot of good indeed.

Walking out of the ground I notice Swiggy, legendary drinker and a man who, hailing from a former pit village near Dudley, has even less time for the Albion than I do. He smiles the smile of a man who started his enjoyment of today very early indeed and intends to carry on for a long time. I doubt he's the only one.

Onto a Metro so crowded I have to get off at the first available opportunity. To the Actress & Bishop, purveyors of fine ales and, on Sunday afternoons, decent music in the shape of drumming Dean Beresford, grandson of former thirties Villa forward Joe, and his ensemble made up of local jazz and blues musicians. A pleasant hour or so and a couple of pints while listening to a fine band rounds off an enjoyable day. Well, I say rounds off but it's still only just gone five o'clock when I get home so I'm in wife Bernie's good books. Early kick-offs aren't all bad.

22nd September: Evening Mail letters column (definitely not home). Albion fans have been let loose with their crayons. "*Rather lose than play like that*" is a predictable response to yesterday's match. Not that they have much choice.

24th September 2008: QPR (home). We played QPR in this competition four years ago and it went off, as I believe the term goes, before and after the match. No police were on duty and they took forever to turn up when it kicked off on Witton Lane after. Sadly, a steward who was caught up in the trouble died, although whether it was connected to the fighting has never been proved. Fortunately tonight's a lot quieter.

It's another of our 'give the reserves a chance' team selections. I'd call it squad rotation but that would imply we have a squad. With Carew, Barry, Young and Petrov in the team we should have enough quality to beat Rangers, but this was a night when nobody seemed too bothered. Marlon Harewood missed the only chance we had in the first half and Jon Carew missed the only one we had after the break. In between we gave away a daft goal from a corner and even the introduction of Gabby Agbonlahor couldn't find us an equaliser.

That's probably our best chance of winning a trophy gone for the season. The League Cup has provided me and the rest of my generation of Villa supporters with some of our finest memories. It was the one trophy we used to think of as 'ours'. Take away the QPR fans and less than 20,000 bothered to turn up tonight on a pleasant evening and a lot of those that were here seemed to shrug their collective shoulders at the end and mutter something about not wanting any fixture congestion. I expect this to be a recurrent theme throughout the season.

26th September: There are several teams I like to see doing well. Crewe, because they're a well-run club with the right idea about bringing young players on. Hereford, because of that cup tie against Newcastle a hundred years ago and also because

Graham Turner's a nice guy and it wasn't his fault he was hopelessly out of his depth when Doug appointed him. Then most of all, whoever Brian Little's managing now. In the past it's been Darlington, Leicester, Stoke and Hull. Obviously not when he was at Albion – blind devotion only stretches so far – and since last season Wrexham. No longer, though, because he's resigned with them midway in the Conference. It only seems five minutes since he was making us title challengers and our only worry was how long we'd have before the FA wanted him to manage England. Now he can't do anything with Wrexham. Management must be a lot harder than I reckon.

27th September: Sunderland (home). With a couple of obvious exceptions I don't think anyone has a bad word to say about Sunderland supporters. They turn up in decent numbers, sing a lot and don't have any of the pretension which accompanies their Geordie neighbours. Plus Mensi, singer with seminal punk band the Angelic Upstarts, is one of them, and as celebrity fans go that's got to be better than Jasper Carrott. The sun's shining, our league form's good, we've got a Saturday three o'clock kick-off and all told it's one of those days when football's the best thing on earth and Villa Park the best place to watch it.

We've got our first team back out. In fact, so first is this team that it's been unchanged for six league games. That doesn't stop them from playing like a bunch of strangers from kick-off, and it was no surprise when Sunderland took the lead after nine minutes. Steed Malbranque, a player we maybe should have taken a closer look at in the summer, played a lovely ball through to Cisse, who hit a good first-time shot past Brad Friedel.

Luckily this woke the Villa up, and another eight minutes later Ashley Young hit a perfectly placed free-kick past Craig Gordon to put us level. The sun continued to beat down, the ball was passed around with aplomb. Things were looking good. They looked even better after 33 minutes, when another free-kick from Ashley Young hit the wall, ricocheted to Stilyan Petrov and his cross was flicked in by John Carew. Then with a couple of minutes left in the first half Gordon made a double stop to prevent first Gabby and then Gareth Barry from getting a third. We wanted to sign Gordon last summer but he preferred to stay closer to his home town of Edinburgh. We got Scott Carson instead. There's a link there about Scottish goalkeepers.

It seems half-time is dragging on forever. If Doug was still in charge we'd probably have put it down to him wanting to maximise the amount spent during the interval but just as I'm about to ask the stewards how long we have to be delayed before we're entitled to a refund the players re-emerge. It later transpires that one of the linesmen, as I still insist on calling them, got injured during the first half. Why it should take fifteen minutes for him to hand his flag and notebook over to the fourth official, God knows.

The second half's a bit scrappy, with Gabby drifting out wide where he can't do so much damage although he did have one long-range shot not far off target. Martin makes one of his regular weird substitutions, Nickey Shorey being replaced by James Milner. Sunderland go close a couple of times, but Martin Laursen and Curtis Davies are starting to look like they can work together. Villa central defenders always have a lot to live up to – we've had some corkers in the past – and this partnership is looking like it could be more than useful. As long as Laursen stays clear of injuries and Davies doesn't do his pub player act too often we'll have nothing to worry about.

There are some Sunderland fans in the Barton's afterwards. They're happy to talk football in the nicely self-deprecating way genuine fans usually are and we all agree what a pity it is that two such fine clubs are spoilt by having such unworthy neighbours. Later General Krulak, on the H&V website, as good as calls the gate disappointing and talks about four thousand empty seats. "*I don't know what else we can do,*" he says. Fair comment, but our gates are at almost an all-time high and maybe for the moment we should be thankful for what we've got.

October

European diplomacy

2nd October: Litex Lovich (home). There was never going to be a problem getting a decent seat for this game so I hung onto my money until the last possible minute and end up in the North Stand as usual, but in the next block. From here we can observe the Bloke Behind Me at distance. The Bloke Behind Me has entered footballing mythology. Everyone has at some stage shared the Bloke's philosophy on life, the game and the useless wankers on the pitch. My own personal Bloke is nice enough, but he does have a tendency to get over-excited at the sight of a referee blowing the whistle to start a football match and can't be calmed down for at least 90 minutes, plus stoppages.

When Litex get a penalty the Bloke goes into a paroxysm of fury, calling upon the Gods to rain thunder down upon the referee and pleading with Brad Guzan to make a save reminiscent of Gordon Banks in 1970. Brad doesn't, Litex equalise and the Bloke's anger steps up several notches. Well we are only two up from the away leg after all.

Before that Marlon Harewood scored a great goal, laid on by a header from Ashley Young. Yes, you read that right. Young headed the ball, Harewood smashed it home like Peter Withe in his prime.

From the unusual to the routine. Martin picked a bunch of fringe players and they've been disappointing. We've got a team that could match any in the league and if we're still in with a shout in a few months time we're going to be relying on the players we had out tonight to do a regular job. But that's another argument, for another time. Litex knew they had no chance of getting through so they've come here for the experience and they certainly seem to have enjoyed themselves. Their group of fans in the Witton Lane downstairs have made a lot of noise, give their countryman Stilyan Petrov a sporting ovation and let's hope they've had a good time in Birmingham. The city's promoting itself as a tourist destination and every little helps.

And so we ease into the group stages of the UEFA Cup. Six European games gone and we're hardly into October. Now we've got another four to qualify for the last 32, which by my reckoning would be four more rounds until the final. If we're going to win the UEFA Cup that'll be 19 games. One of the reasons the Premier League was set up was to reduce the number of league games and therefore help the national side. Roaring success, then.

On the way home I saw a gang of kids wearing Villa shirts in a chippy. Going to a night match then finishing off with a bag of chips – doesn't that remind you of when you were a kid? I hope they still do batters.

5th October: Chelsea (away). It's cheap to go to London on Sunday with Chiltern. When you're off to Chelsea it's the only thing that is cheap.

Writing about a visit to Stamford Bridge is easy; the hell-hole it used to be, players like Doug Rougvie and Vinnie Jones, the supporters they used to have, and comparisons with what they've become. But the fact remains that Chelsea, more than any other club, ground or set of supporters, are typical of what football has evolved into. What was once nasty, often squalid and sometimes dangerous is now safety-conscious big business. You're not going to get beaten up at Stamford Bridge any more, but you are going to pay a lot of money, more than you would once have ever dreamed possible, to see your team play there. Whether you think that's an improvement depends on your mentality, probably your age and upbringing as well and, I guess, the size of your wallet.

On the way down I get talking to a group who get on the train at Leamington. They're the sort you see everywhere, say hello to and know nothing about. They're good enough company for the hour and a bit we're on the train, but I know that for all their dedication to the Villa they'll never feel like I do, or Mac, Dave Woodley, Greg and all of us around the country who followed our team in the old days. Away travel now is about booking tickets in advance, eating at an American-franchised burger bar, going into the officially-designated away pub to drink whatever fizzy liquid has the biggest advertising budget this quarter, singing the same songs every other set of fans sings with just the words changed, then heading back to the station for the first train home. Their thinking is done for them and I know I'm qualifying for Grumpy Old Man status.

I'm in no mood for touring West London today – it's a strictly straight in, straight out mission. Get off at Marylebone, walk to Edgware Road (quicker than getting the tube then changing), tube to Fulham Broadway. Into the ground, watch the Villa become the first team to win at Stamford Bridge since the Ice Age, home again. Sorted, as I believe young people say.

We're third in the league and kidded ourselves we've got a chance this afternoon. Not only that but seasoned pundits, and Mark Lawrenson, reckon we could be the team to finally beat Chelsea. If only real life were like the script.

Last season was that memorable 4-4 draw at Christmas when we were two up before Zat Knight got sent off and ended up equalising in injury time, Gareth Barry scoring a penalty when Chelsea were down to nine men. My predictions are always wrong and several grateful bookmakers will happily confirm the fact, but I'd put money on this afternoon being nothing like that one.

The tube's full of tourists getting off at Notting Hill hoping to see Hugh Grant plus a few nouveau Chelsea fans who regard him as a role model. Eventually I roll off at Fulham Broadway, which since the last time I was here has been turned into a plush shopping centre. I can well imagine the ICF and Headhunters going toe to toe outside Starbuck's. Actually, Stamford Bridge is the one ground in London where I've never seen any problems. I don't deny that it could have been a right evil place to visit, but in the old days we never played a game here that was important enough to bring more than a few hundred supporters so we slipped under their radar. Chelsea also spent a few spells in the second division, believe it or not.

We could go top if we win and as the two teams come out we're full of confidence, especially as Chelsea are missing four or five top names. Every successful team needs a high-profile victory to announce themselves – Liverpool at home in the championship season or the opening day 3-1 against Manchester United in 1995 for example. Everyone in the away section of what is still the Shed, whatever name it might be given, is convinced that today will be the day the class of 2009 come of age. Then Chris Foy blew his whistle and the day went downhill...

We had our arses kicked. Men against boys and all that. There's no shame in losing to the best and today Chelsea were as good as it gets. We were two down at half-time and they could have had six. Talking to Dave Hodges, another of our supporters who doesn't miss a game – ever – we were joking that this could have been a score from the good old days of Billy McNeill but luckily Chelsea weren't as good at scoring goals as making them so 2-0 at the end it was. You know Match of the Day will be doing it in its communal trousers this evening and Lawro will forget he tipped us to win, but at least we got away relatively unharmed.

I missed the six o'clock train back from Marylebone, the half pasts are always full of shoppers going home to High Wycombe so it was the seven o'clock. At three minutes to I was congratulating myself on choosing a relatively quite carriage. A minute later I was in the middle of a group of fine upstanding youth who passed the time between Marylebone and my merciful release at Solihull debating the relative merits of Nietzsche's Superman theory and its relevance to modern post-industrial society.

My Chelsea-supporting author colleague James Clarke reckons that's the best they've played for three years. It's not much of a consolation.

11th October: More proof that loyalty in football is strictly, accruing to everyone in football, a one-way thing. Ashley Cole is booed during England's game with Kazakhstan. The reaction from the press is as if the world's come to an end. It's okay for them to pile derision on Sir Graham and every other England manager, or to moan about players who under-perform. But when we, the paying punters, tell a highly-paid prima donna what we think of him, that's unacceptable.

18th October: Portsmouth (home). You always associate certain clubs with certain things and the things I associate with Portsmouth are rain, getting beat and early kick-offs. We managed to escape them all with a dry three o'clock 0-0 draw that provided nothing to remember except the sight of Marlon Harewood showing 37,660 people there might still be hope for them to get a game in the Premier League. That might be exaggerating a bit, and Marlon's an easy target, but he's just not good enough. After seven league games with the same team Martin gives James Milner his full league debut and he showed some promise, but Gabby and John Carew didn't hit it off – again. Carlos Cuellar also started, at right back with Luke Young on the bench. There's two minutes to go when Young comes on for Martin Laursen, and Cuellar went to his rightful position. I'd love to know what reasoning Martin uses when he makes substitutions. Maybe we should debate it during the second half of goalless draws, instead of wondering what became of eighties soap stars. If anyone's got any idea what became of Terry Sullivan's wife off Brookside, let us know. Mac reckons she works in Merry Hill Debenhams. Rich reckons Mac's on glue.

Once more it becomes obvious with far too much time left that any team who come to Villa Park wanting to keep the point they started off with will more often than not get their way. If our threat at corners is dealt with and Ashley Young isn't on form, chances are we won't score. Until we get that sorted out we'll drop too many points to ever really threaten the leaderboard. I was never a great fan of Paul Merson but how we need someone with his guile now. John Carew hit the crossbar in stoppage time, and that was about all there was to talk about. Luckily for the inhabitants of the press box, though, they managed to find something to fill their blank columns.

Games with Portsmouth bring the pantomime villain into town, in the shape of Harry Redknapp. I don't know why so many have got it in for him – he's always spoken very highly of us and was injured in the car accident during Italia 90 that killed his mate, former Villa captain Brian Tiler. Maybe it's because football now is so bland that anyone with a bit of personality automatically has to be a bad guy. Whatever, he got his customary booing throughout the match then as the final whistle blew some piece of plankton lobbed a 50p piece at him but hit the linesman. Police launch an inquiry and immediately rule out a grey-haired octogenarian seen in the approximate area of where the coin was thrown, on the grounds that he'd have asked for the 50p back.

That was our last league game at home before the clocks go back. Winter's on its way, which is usually when the injuries and suspensions start to take their toll. How we'll cope remains to be seen.

23rd October: Ajax (home). Some names in football command respect, and tonight's visitors are one of them. They may not have the names of old; Cruyff, Neeskens, Davids or Kluivert, but there's still a sense of anticipation that this could be a Great European Night. Walking down the touchline will be one of the greatest names never to grace this pitch, Ajax coach Marco van Basten. I'm sure that even though he's played in the best venues all over the world, he knows that only tonight will his footballing education be complete.

Before then, we get a taste of what football used to be like in England, and what it's turned into since the days when Villa were European regulars. Back in those halcyon days, few away fans came to Villa Park for European games. The only ones who turned up in anything like numbers were Juventus, most of whom seemed to be Italian restaurateurs living here, and Bilbao, the noisiest and best fans we've ever welcomed. The rest were like Inter – 80,000 for the leg over there, a couple of dozen travelling. Cheap flights and the fact that English grounds are now a lot safer than they used to be, means that most European clubs bring decent followings with them. Maybe not so many with the clubs we've played so far this season, but the 'notorious' Dutch promised to be a bit lively. And so it proved, as while I was talking to a couple of their younger supporters about football then and now, in the company of Dave Woodley who's seen it all, a commotion could be heard from the general direction of Station Road. Around 70 or so Dutch lads were being marched towards the ground by almost that many police, testament to their reputation and the fact that West Midlands' finest never pass up an opportunity to show their strength. As they get to the junction of Witton Lane the police stop them, which is an excuse for the ones at the back to begin jumping up and down, and pushing forward. A couple of Peelers get jostled but it's all over in seconds, nothing to report here and they're marched into the ground. However, you just know what's coming next.

A minute later my phone rings. It's one of the local press corps, namely Lisa 'Hold the Front Page' Smith from the Mail. "*We've heard it's gone off on Witton Lane,*" she says. I put her straight and she's shrewd enough to know that two slightly inconvenienced policemen do not a riot make.

The Dutch lads I was talking to are still there. "*That's not our firm,*" one of them informs me. "*The firm is not travelling. They will be going to Hamburg.*" I wish he'd told the police because even though the Ajax non-firm (the Ajax flaccid?) are now inside the ground and Witton Lane has gone back to its normal pre-match calm their vans remain, revving up and blocking the road. It's ruining the ozone layer, and it's doing neither my sales nor any asthma I may have any good either. I didn't know whether to sue for loss of earnings or industrial injury.

The match got off to a fine start thanks to the Young-Laursen set-piece combination proving deadly once more, and we looked like a team who would impress the watching Euro-millions. Then the watching audience learned that Villa are incapable of going a game without giving away at least one daft goal and we gifted Ajax an equaliser. The thousand or so of their supporters in the lower away bit were going absolutely mental. I had to laugh when they started up with "*You're not singing anymore.*" It's a bit more original than that song about you've never won the European Cup which, sure enough, gets an airing tonight. Ironically, I hope.

For ten minutes they knocked the ball around like the Ajax of old, but just on half-time Gareth Barry thundered in a second for us. He's got the knack of doing the right thing at the right time and he's killed the game off tonight. Martin Laursen and Nicky Shorey missed a couple of chances but the second half was a bit of an anti-climax. Ajax weren't up to much, we did enough to win and the atmosphere was definitely not Great European Night, no matter how hard we tried. It won't stop grandchildren being bored rigid in fifty years time about the night Villa beat The Mighty Ajax though.

24th October: Another scoop for the press. John Carew was in the Rocket Club (a lap dancing establishment, and don't pretend you didn't know that already) into the wee small hours before last night's match. It's no big deal, but he should have more sense.

26th October: Wigan (away). Last season we took thousands up here thanks to a combination of Christmas and cheap tickets. This season the tickets aren't so cheap and it isn't Christmas so there won't be as much of a travelling army. There might be even less of one than expected as there's a mega hold-up on the M6, caused by an accident. There's always hold-ups on the M6 caused by accidents. It should be bigger, but only the bit going past Manchester is considered important enough for four lanes. University theses could be written on Brummie paranoia with regards to the second city argument. I've been sitting there for half an hour reading my paper and nothing's moved. Rich, who lives in Lancashire and is travelling behind me after a night out in Birmingham, rings to say he's knackered and won't risk trying to make up for lost time so he's heading straight home. Others further behind must be tempted to turn back or find a pub.

Just when I'm at the point of resigning myself to missing the kick-off, things start to move and eventually I arrive on the outskirts of Wigan in time to get caught up in the matchday traffic us early arrivers usually miss.

Last season the wind and rain were so bad that I was perfectly dry standing behind a wall and got soaked running the 50 yards to the turnstiles. Today's better but it does start to rain about five minutes before kick-off. I'm convinced Wigan's jinxed, so I move inside the ground. The pitch is better than it used to be.

Carew's on the bench and Agbonlahor's up front in a 4-5-1 formation. I'm never keen on playing like this, but it seems to suit Gabby. He won us a penalty after being fouled by Titus Bramble (who's such an easy target I'm not saying another word) and generally gave the Wigan defence the runaround in an open first half where the home side had a couple of chances as well. That Wilson Palacios looks a good player, you couldn't imagine any club he signed for ever letting him go without making serious money on him. Unless of course they were really, really stupid.

Half-time, and I overhear one of those delightful conversations which say so much about the youth of today as Wigan's goalkeeping coach Nigel Spink knocks a ball around with their substitute goalkeeper.

"*What we clapping that fat twat for?*"

"*Because he's Nigel Spink.*"

"*Who?*"

I amble along through the concourse (if the JD stadium is deserving of such a title), where I bump into Greg, who's just arrived after being stuck in the M6 jam. "*At least it meant I could park at that shopping place. I'll be here less than two hours.*" It's a consolation and it keeps him happy.

Back to my seat for the second half and no sooner does it get started than Barry's in a collision with some clogging northerner (even if he is probably from Eastern Europe) and off to be replaced by John Carew. It's a bold, even reckless, move by Martin to replace a midfielder with a striker when we're a goal up away from home, but it pays off almost immediately. Carew's first touch is a flick on to Gabby, who scores our second and makes sure of the points. That's why Martin's the manager.

Five minutes later Agbonlahor returns the favour, as they say in all the best match reports, and Carew puts us three up. Do players really think like that? Would Gabby have thought "*I'll have to pass to him, I owe him one*"?

We go through the full repertoire of John Carew lapdancing classics, Martin make another of his strange substitutions when Luke Young is replaced by Zat Knight, and with five minutes to go Steve Sidwell replaces the ever-improving Stilyan Petrov. I like Sidwell and I hope his form will pick up. The goal he got in stoppage time will help.

4-0 away, against a team no less an expert than Tony Cascarino tipped as an outside bet to break into the top four. Yes, I know. But a four goal away win's not to be sneezed at, especially against a team managed by King Edwardface. Anyone who's at Small Heath long enough (about five minutes will usually do) is bound to be contaminated by their hatred of us and do all within their power to stop us.

On the way home I ponder the pros and cons of Wigan avoiding relegation.

Pros:

Their existence in the Premier League annoys many people.

It's cheap to get in.

Thousands of available tickets.

The probability of Stuart Hall doing the summarising.

We've won there twice in a row.

Jeff Stelling announcing Wigan v Hull as a fixture in the greatest league in the world.

Cons:

The weather.

I always have some sort of problem here.

The M6.

Listening to Radio Manchester.

No matter when we play them there will always be Manchester United and Liverpool supporters travelling in the same direction.

29th October: Blackburn (home). We always seem to play Blackburn midweek, although if I check back it's probably been about ten years since it happened. We used to play Wednesday night league games regularly back in the days when every winter would see loads of postponements and we had things like cup runs to concern us, but global warming has seen the end of both those phenomena. Just as well, because they were usually 2-0 defeats to Middlesbrough in front of 18,000. I'm sure we played Middlesbrough on a Friday night once because of the Motor Show, but nobody remembers it or whether it's true. You ponder these things while standing on Witton Lane when there's hardly anyone around.

Paul Ince was one of those players about who you wondered how he hadn't been sussed out long ago. For all his reputation as a hard man he was never around when the players who could really handle themselves were on the opposition and where was he in the Euro 96 penalty shoot-out? Hiding behind Gareth Southgate. The job he did with Macclesfield and Franchise FC entitled him to a crack at a bigger club, but straight from there to the Premier League is proving too big a step.

Roque Santa Cruz is yet another player who gets injured in the warm-up. What's going on here? In the old days players trained all week on Woodbines and Guinness, then ran around for five minutes before the match with a bloke who had a bucket of cold water and a sponge shouting at them. I can't remember any problems until the players kicked off. Now they're fitter than Olympic athletes, it's only a matter of time before a team comes onto the pitch trailing an entire operating theatre behind them (my money's on Chelsea), yet they're always falling over before the kick-off.

Blackburn to their credit have some nice touches and it's no surprise when they go a goal up after half an hour. Naturally the goal was made by Benni McCarthy, the man chased by John Gregory like a lovesick schoolgirl what seems an eternity ago. Villa have the ability to make hard work of games like this and we could really do with some inspiration from somewhere. It's more divine than man-made when it does arrive; Luke Young has two attempts to get the ball over the line with almost the last kick of the first half.

Midway through the second half and we've improved just enough to be on top when James Milner chases what looks to be a hopeless cause to the byeline. If it had been Ashley Young the Rovers defence might have been a bit more alert, but nobody in the ground expected Milner to get the ball until he did, and he centred for Gareth Barry to put us into the lead.

Carew's on and we're starting to look a bit more like a decent team. Ashley Young starts off a nice move with three minutes to go, which leads to Gabby getting yet another goal. That should have made the win certain but the defence are mentally already getting changed when Rovers pull a goal back with a couple of minutes stoppage time left. They don't get the ball into our half after that so it wasn't a costly error but that's not the point. For years we've been able to rely on our defence and now it's, er, unreliable. Whether Olof Mellberg's departure or the problems we've had with full-backs is the cause I don't know, but we're letting in some daft goals. When in doubt blame Doug is the best policy in such matters. But that's three wins in a week, we're fourth in the league and it might not last so enjoy it while you can. Paul Ince doesn't look like he'll be enjoying it for much longer. It truly could not happen to a more deserving case.

November

The good, the bad and the drowned rat

3rd November: Newcastle United (away). Have you ever looked at the fixtures in the lower divisions, seen, for example, Darlington away at Brighton on a Tuesday night and wondered which clown thought that one up? Believe it or not, the clubs at that level ask for their longer journeys midweek because it means they don't have an overnight stop or have to start out at six on Saturday morning. This is not a factor which should influence TV channels when they give us a pleasant 400-mile round trip for a Monday night - again. I make my protest by not going up there (therefore not using fossil fuels and doing my bit for the planet) and not watching on Sky (striking back against globalisation) either.

It's just before nine o'clock before I get the chance to listen to what's going on. I'm driving home, nil-nil and Five Live say nothing much has happened. Switch over to WM and they reckon Villa have had a couple of good chances. With Newcastle unreliable at home and the Tooners bound to start getting on their team's collective back if they don't score soon I'm in a confident mood. Twenty minutes later things have changed completely. Joey Barton's decided he's a footballer, Villa can't cope and Newcastle are a goal up. Daz Hale and Mark Regan on WM are ranting away about Villa's lack of everything. I like WM and tend not to take much notice of the claims that they, like the Mail, are part of some enormous Midlands media conspiracy against the Villa. But I do wish they'd stop trying to be impartial and remember that they're a local station for local people. Soon afterwards it's two-nil, Alan Green says Villa seem to have given up and to be honest, from what I'm hearing it's hard to disagree. Later reports from eye-witnesses indicate that some of the team seem tired already, which at the beginning of November is a worry.

At just after two in the morning I'm woken up by rain on the window, look at the clock and realise I probably wouldn't be home yet if I'd gone to the match. As I drift back off to sleep my last conscious thought is that being a part-time fan has the odd consolation.

6th November: Slavia Prague (away). I toyed with breaking my self-imposed European away ban for this one. Nice city, plenty to do, they're used to dealing with English tourists (which is, admittedly, a mixed blessing) and the Villa are playing there. It sounds perfect, but I think the bottom line is that these days I'm just too downright idle to go through all the procedures of getting flights, hotels and match tickets. Internet talk before the game centred on meeting at somewhere called the Stella bar, which is apparently one of the most expensive places in the city. Anyone going to Prague and drinking Stella out of choice deserves all the ripping-off they get, but it appears a fine old time was had by all.

Those of us watching on Channel Five had a bit of a surprise when the line-up was announced. It's time to rest a few first-teamers again, with Brad Guzan and Moustapha Salifou starting. This time they're looking impressive, unlike their previous appearances. Steve Sidwell's shot is deflected into the net by John Carew with the rest of the team growing in confidence. Second half sees Slavia attacking and the outstanding performers are Guzan and Salifou, who really does look the part as he wins ball after ball in midfield. Maybe he isn't crap after all.

What wasn't noticeable on TV were the scuffles that broke out between some heavy-handed stewards and a few of our supporters, but luckily they were over almost as soon as they began. Not a great performance, but a valuable lesson learned about coping with pressure in a faraway land. We won, making qualification for the knockout stages virtually assured and the trip to Hamburg isn't as important as it might have seemed.

9th November: Middlesbrough (home). If we weren't in the UEFA Cup we'd have played the day before. The weather was okay then and we always sell more of a new issue on Saturdays. Instead we're stuck with a Sunday and gathering storm clouds. Just turned half past one and it started raining. Well, I say raining in the same way I say Robert Mugabe can be a bit over-zealous. It hammered down incessantly until kick-off, by which time I'd long since given my sellers instructions to abandon ship if they so desired. Mac and Percy, standing undercover, manfully clung to the posts until the Aston Lifeboat was launched but some of the others – mentioning no names as knowing the shame will live with them until the grave is sufficient punishment for their black souls – took the feeble excuse of imminent drowning to head for the comparative comfort of the ground.

One up front again with Carlos Cuellar at right-back and Petrov missing so Steve Sidwell's making his first league start. He, like every player on the pitch, does nothing of much note for half an hour until Nicky Shorey's cock up provides Tuncay with the opportunity to put Boro in the lead. Three minutes later James Milner crosses to give Sidwell his second league goal in a fortnight.

It's a crap game and the rain's still blowing in, one of those when a team of honest, stout-hearted English yeomen will always prevail against foreign mercenaries such as Boro have filled their team with. Or put another way, neither team seem arsed trying to win. Brad Friedel spills a shot and Boro's Afonso Alves conjours up a miss of Ronnie Rosenthalian proportions. He gets substituted straight after and if that was why he didn't score I don't blame him. If I was as rich as a Premier League footballer I might be tempt to think going off ten minutes early was worth missing out on a win bonus in these conditions. He needn't have worried because with three minutes to go Steve Sidwell makes sure the result matches the weather by sliding an attempted back-pass which only reaches Tuncay and we're not going to get two let-offs in the same match.

It's raining, we've lost and I can't be bothered to stand by the bus stop hearing a dozen would-be Peter Kays thinking they're the first ones to ever say "*They'm all bluddy Villains*" so it's straight out, beat the traffic and away. Squelching into the Barton's I reflect on the glamour of the Premier League and whether I will ever be dry again.

I've had better days.

15th November: Arsenal (away). As Northern Soul legend Chuck Wood sang, and Dexy's later covered, seven days is too long. Good job it was only six between last Sunday's thoroughly miserable affair and our visit to the Emirates. This is our third trip to Arsenal's new home and we've yet to lose here. In fact we deserved to win both our previous visits, with the Gunners getting undeserved late equalisers on both occasions.

There's a choice of tube stations, and indeed tube lines, to get to Arsenal, so there's plenty of places for pre-match entertainment. This is one of the joys of London; ten minutes on the tube and you can be in an area where there's no thought of football and consequently no queues for anything, least of all chemical-smelling lager served in plastic glasses. Today's choice of venue is the Lamb's Conduit, close to Great Ormond Street Hospital. There's about seven other people in there and it seems from overhearing another conversation that five of us live within a mile of each other. Don't you hate it when strangers overhear you?

It's a very nice pub serving very nice beer and a pity to leave it but needs must. The underground station's round the corner, four stops away is Arsenal and therefore it's less than half an hour from bar to turnstiles. The route from tube station to the ground is always impressive. There are so many stalls set out it's more like a street market than the approach to a football ground. No wonder Arsenal fanzines sell so many copies; there's a real pre-match culture of wandering around looking at what's on offer. At Villa Park there's nothing apart from a handful of badge sellers and burger vans so supporters walk from wherever they've been straight into the ground. Yes, I am envious.

Arsenal have not only what is architecturally the best ground built in Britain since 1897 they've also, just about, remembered they're still a football club. It's one of the few places that allow us to sell close to the turnstiles even if last season an over-enthusiastic policewoman demanded to know what, who and where I was selling. It's not 1989 anymore, these fanzine things have been around for a few years. You may have come across one of them before. No such problems today although one Arsenal supporter did walk past and hurled the most cutting insult he could think of: "*I hope you lose five nil.*" Wounding, that one. I hope they've run out of chocolate sprinkles for his cappuccino.

It's a good view from all parts of the Emirates, even if I do wish I could sit down. I'm as in favour of terraces as anyone, but sometimes I wish those who insist on standing up all through the game would realise that a lot of us don't sit at away games because we want to, but because if we didn't all we'd see would be the back of whoever's stood in front.

What I didn't expect to see was 45 minutes of dominance spoilt only by a worrying inability to put the ball in the net. We even manage to miss a penalty, which is only partly explained by the fact that Gareth Barry couldn't take it as he was off the field when it was given.

Half-time is that familiar all-the-play-but-no-goals mixture of pleasure and apprehension. Arsenal can't be this bad in the second half and they've got a worrying record of equalising against us down here. It's at times like this I could do with Percy and his often annoying but in this instance reassuring brand of manic optimism. Unfortunately Percy's phobia of London almost rivals that of Tom Ross and the closest he'll get to this afternoon's match is watching Euston trains pull into International.

The second half gets underway with a resigned fatalism that lasts about eight seconds until I realise this is no illusion, Villa are still going to dominate the match. The crowd are getting restless, which means that either the canapés have run out or they've realised it's not going to be Arsenal's afternoon. Agbonlahor and Young are tearing a new hole in the Arsenal defence, as our uncouth American cousins would describe it, but there's still no score until 20 minutes to go, when Ashley's cross is so perfect that Arsenal defender Clichy has two options – score himself or let Gabby do it. He takes the first option and it's one-nil. Arsenal and their supporters are complaining that one of their defenders has been on the floor when we attacked. Arsene Wenger will have seen that one alright.

As expected they throw everything at us and ten minutes later, as expected, there's a goal. To us. Martin Laursen lashes the ball out of defence, it falls nicely for Gabby, who races past Gallas and hits the back of the net from the edge of the box.

We have ten minutes of friendly abuse towards the retreating backs of the Arsenal fans, until the referee brings an end to one of the most unexpectedly enjoyable 90 minutes of football I've seen for a long while. We've taken on a team who, and I'll say this as I'm in a good mood, play the game as well as any, and beaten them not by luck or holding on against the odds but by being better than they were.

As we're jubilantly herded out of the ground I realise this is no time to be rushing for the first train home. I spy a couple of fellow Barton's regulars in the shape of Barry Rose and his uncle, and insist they join me in my celebrations. Barry lives in London but he's still not participated in the city's finest mini-pub crawl, along High Holborn from the Cittie of Yorke via the Penderel's Oak to the Princess Louise. The first of these is a Tudor ale house with original booths (well, maybe not exactly dating back to the Spanish Armada, but close enough) and barrels made into tables. There's a trick you can play to someone on their first visit here – get them to buy the first round. They assume that because it's not far from the West End and such an obvious tourist trap they'll need a second mortgage, when in fact it's Sam Smith's northern prices and three pints is not much more than a fiver.

We move on to the Penderel's, a Wetherspoon house but one of the best of that bunch. Barry, thinking his luck can't last, insists on paying. Some time later we finish off at the Princess Louise, another fine example of public house architecture. Smith's again, same prices. Barry can't believe this is the same city where he lives, his uncle thinks he's in a timeslip. Villa have won at Arsenal and we're paying less than two quid a pint. It must be 1993 again.

I leave them to it. I've got a train to catch and the last one out of Marylebone is traditionally the pisshead special so I'd rather be long gone before then.

Realising I haven't eaten for nearly twelve hours I head for the pasty stall. The nice lady there is offloading ready to close for the night so she gives me a couple of bonuses. Free food, cheap beer and three unexpected points.

I've had worse days.

19th November: I don't take much notice of internationals, but it's always good to see Villa players getting into the England team, just so we can keep hold of the record for most England players. Gabby Agbonlahor is the latest and while I'm pleased for him and for us, I can't help but look back to the days when Dennis Mortimer, Gary Shaw and the rest of their colleagues failed to get a single cap. Also of minor interest is the Serbia v Bulgaria match. Stilyan Petrov is in the Bulgarian side, while making his debut for Serbia, after playing 102 times for the old Serbia & Montenegro, is our old mate Savo Milosevic. I used to like him when he was at Villa, even if a badly-edited interview after he had his fall-out at Blackburn meant I came across as saying something different. One man spent several months after that shouting at me that I'd "*got Savo the sack.*" If I'd had so much influence over Villa's transfer policy we'd have signed Alan Shearer and anyway, I doubt Savo spent much time in the Jobcentre. He was a strange character, Savo. Massively talented but woefully slow to react. You could hear him thinking, as one writer put it, and it didn't take much – a hard tackle, a throw-in given the wrong way – to have him raising his hands to the skies as if this was just one more in a long line of injustices handed down to his people over the centuries and he could do nothing but suffer in their name.

22nd November: Manchester United (home). Things about the match I hate, in no particular order. 1) November, 2) 5.30 kick offs, 3) Man United at home. Put them all together and you get a recipe for misery.

Witton Lane is as friendly as it usually is when this lot are in town. There's touts, wannabe gangsters, drunks and a host of daytrippers cluttering up the pavements. It's supposedly illegal to tout tickets and drink in the streets, but I've never seen anyone arrested outside Villa Park for either offence.

A lot of internet posters complain that Manchester United fans get away with standing throughout the games and being in the home sections. I don't particularly have a problem with either – we boast about standing at our own away matches and if our part-time fans can't be bothered to get tickets in time that's their look out. I get more worked up about the inevitability of this fixture ever since Alan Hansen said that thing about kids 12 years ago. We hold them for a bit, they step up a gear, bring on two players who would play every game for us and get two late goals. But this season we're showing that maybe, just maybe, things might be different. Last week's win at Arsenal will have boosted our confidence while their bench looks short of match-winners.

There's not a lot to get worked up about with our defence doing well to hold back United when they attack. Normally their running off the ball is something even their worst enemy would applaud, but they seem off the pace today. Maybe November is having an effect, or it could even be that we're raising our game.

At half time there's a lot of "*They're bound to come at us in the second half.*" Playing United is about psychology as much as their superior talent. I'm sure a lot of teams don't try to attack because they'd rather lose 2-0 than risk annoying them so they'll score five or six. This would explain some of our performances, although it was probably O'Leary's tactic against everyone else as well. We couldn't compete with the Charltons of this world, after all.

We had a decent shout for a penalty in the second half but this is Manchester United we're playing so it wasn't really worth wasting the energy. Tevez goes off, Nani comes on. Ronaldo is substituted for Anderson. Usually it would be the other way round and that's proof we've mastered them.

The final whistle blows on a 0-0 draw, our first point against United since 2002, and it's started raining. After-match sales are surprisingly good, which means we're pleased with the draw that takes us above Arsenal, who've also drawn, into fourth place. In a couple of years time we might see it as two points dropped but for now let's take heart from the fact that we didn't capitulate against Manchester United, at times we even attacked them and the world didn't come to an end.

The good news is that we've got Man United at home and most of November out of the way. 5.30 kick-offs are a bit harder to get rid of.

23rd November: We're round the house of Jo, her two children and their idiot husband/father Greg, a man so obsessed with adding to his collection of Villa memorabilia he once asked Doug to sign a copy of the club accounts. He's got an idea. Drive to Hamburg early on matchday, come straight back and that way it's cheap and doesn't need much time off work. Permission is asked from the heads of both households and granted provided we don't ask for spending money and we bring back presents.

28th November: That lot over the city are usually good for a laugh on their own but today they've got a bit of help, and it's no less a personage than Mike Whitby, leader of the council and a man you'd think would know better. He says that to raise the city's profile we should change our name to Aston Villa Birmingham. He really **should** know better – there's not a Villa supporter I've come across who gives a toss about *"bearing the city's name"* but every one of the underclass will have you believe it's more important than any trophy you could win. Taking their one self-announced claim to fame away would be like stripping a man of all his dignity.

29th November. Fulham (home). Fulham are now regulars in the Premier League but without checking I can only remember two games against them at Villa Park. There was last season, when a Shaun Maloney goal deep into injury time gave us a win we scarcely deserved and before that they came to Villa Park when they were in the third division for an FA Cup tie in 1999. Stan Collymore stormed out of the ground before kick-off and we lost. I can't remember any more – isn't that appalling? It's a good job I don't have to do anything important like write about football.

Fulham haven't won at Villa in the league for 35 years and they've only got two points away from home all season. This of course means only one thing – a turgid 0-0 draw with a couple of chances for Barry and only Ashley Young doing anything to remember. John Carew's out injured so it's one up front again, which is going to win us no friends. The game's crying out all through the second half for a change of direction but there isn't anyone capable of coming on and doing it so the same eleven finish as started. With our only attacking threat on the bench the untried Nathan Delfouneso or the very much tried Marlon Harewood there probably wasn't much point. It could have been the first game in living memory to witness no substitutes, but with five minutes to go Fulham bring on Zoltan Gera to waste a bit of time so even that potentially noteworthy incident never happened.

Two home games in a row and two goalless draws. If the first proved we can compete with the best, this one shows we can also be stopped a bit too easily. We could have gone third if we'd won tonight. That 'if' word might be heard a bit more before the season's out.

30th November: Today's the FA Cup third round draw. It's changed beyond all recognition since it used to take place on Monday dinnertime. You'd turn on Radio Two at half past twelve where they'd go live to Lancaster Gate just in time to hear the chairman of the meeting say "*And now to the next item on the agenda, the draw for the third round of the FA Challenge Cup.*" You'd wonder what could be higher on any agenda than the cup draw. Then you'd hear Villa get drawn against Liverpool or Arsenal away, and you knew that in the background Bert Millichip had stuck a hanky in his mouth so no-one could hear him sniggering. His one big regret was that he couldn't draw us away to Moscow Dinamo. Now the fun's gone out of it and we just get Man United all the time. Today's slightly different. We get Stockport, in Greater Manchester. Or Gillingham. It's still away though.

December

Villa are on the telly again

4th December: MSK Zilina (home). Ah, the glamour of European football. We're playing a team no-one knows a thing about (unless you spend too much time watching football on TV than is good for you), and half an hour before kick-off there's about as many people walking up Witton Lane as you get for a later-rounds Youth Cup tie. Zalina have brought a few supporters, and they've made their presence heard outside. Not in an Ajax try-so-hard-to-be-tough way, but by singing and enjoying themselves. Good luck to them.

It's a cup match so the squad players are in, with eight changes from the team who played Fulham. I've been severely under-impressed by the attitude of some of our fringe players when they've had the chance this season. Moustapha Salifou and Isiah Osbourne, to name but two, should be busting a gut to prove they deserve a chance in the first team but no.

Sixteen minutes gone and Zat Knight appears to duck out of a header which gives the visitors the lead. Three minutes later and they're carving through our defence to go two up. This isn't part of the script. Their supporters are naturally enough going mad at what they're watching. We're the world-famous Aston Villa, former European Cup winners, and they're battering us.

Nathan Delfouneso pulls one back after 28 minutes and to be fair to Marlon, it was his work that laid on the goal. This is more like it. You've had your fun, little club. Your supporters have enjoyed themselves. Now accept your beating and have a nice visit to London tomorrow. Give the Queen our regards and tell

Wills how good his team's ground is.

As the game wore on Milner and Barry replaced Salifou and Osbourne with Agbonlahor replacing Delfouneso with 15 mins to go. It's all to no avail and the amount of misplaced passes and crosses either hitting the first defender or going out for a throw reaches epidemic proportions. Chances are missed, and this is the earliest in any season we're relying on updates from the nearest available radio. Luckily Hamburg are two up against Slavia so there's not as much despondency as there could be.

Craig Gardner hits the post with seconds remaining and as the final whistle goes the Zilina (it's an industrial centre with a population of 85,000) fans are hailing their club's famous victory. Fortunately the other result went for us so we're through to the knockout stages, albeit in third place which means we'll be playing a group winner rather than a third place team or Champions League cast-off. Whether that's a lucky break or just papering over the cracks remains to be seen.

7th December: Everton (away). Everton's always been one of my favourite away games. There aren't many proper football grounds left in the Premier League, much less ones still surrounded by rows of terraced houses. You can imagine years ago a whole row of old blokes in flat caps leaving the house, shutting the front door and marching in line over the road to Goodison. You can also imagine they were the sort of idealistic patriots who marched in line to join up in 1914 and never went to Goodison, or indeed home, ever again. I can see why they need to move ground, but I hope they never do. The fact that an Everton free of debt and able to pull in 50,000 regularly are the sort of club who could seriously threaten us is another reason.

I hadn't driven up to Goodison for years and my old parking space is now residents only so it's either pay in a car park – the very idea – or drive round until I can find somewhere I won't get a ticket. The latter option is always best even on Merseyside, and luckily we find a promising spot not too far from that set of traffic lights at the end of the East Lancs road. My passengers, Percy and his mate whose name I never can remember, moan about the walk but I point out that a ten minute walk's better than waiting in traffic for an hour and once we're past those lights the road is always clear. They still moan.

Inside the ground and the view's not bad. A few rows back and level with the penalty area, which is better than a lot of the seats in here. Villa Park used to have the highest number of obstructed view seats in the country until we demolished the old Trinity Road, Goodison must hold the record now.

As it's an away game and I've not been standing outside the ground for hours I can witness that rarity for me, a kick off. Just as well because we've scored one of the best goals of the season within a minute when James Milner gets the ball, lays off neatly to Steve Sidwell and our ginger destroyer smashes home from 20 yards. Quite a few of our supporters have missed the goal and come running from downstairs to join the celebrations. Serves them right, fancy not being here at the start.

They'd missed the best bit of the game as well, as our midfield went missing and it was only a patched-up defence performing heroically that kept Brad Friedel from being worked to death. Everton get an equaliser (I'd say deserved but stuff that) and it's down to the palatial concourse of the Bullens Rd stand.

There's nothing left to eat. I remember those old pork pie things they used to sell here but never seemed to get bought. Did I imagine them or did nobody ever eat one and survive? Some old style football ground catering was definitely best consigned to the past – anyone who ever watched a match north of the border and tried the concoction they called Scotch pies would agree. What kind of animal is a Scotch anyway? Looking at their eggs they must be strange creatures indeed.

Everton live on the telly is the sort of away that brings out the hardcore and the old-school fan, there's no playing up in the pubs then marching down the road singing here and I spend what's left of half-time reminiscing to like minds about times gone by, when getting away from Everton was a case of keeping eyes open and head down. I've seen more trouble at Goodison than any other away ground. The nastiest was the 1984 League Cup semi-final where someone could have died in the running battles and pub wrecking that was going off before and after, the funniest was after the last game of the 1995-96 season, when from a perfect vantage point on the other side of the road I could see some of our lads and their lads walking towards a junction where they bumped into each other and both mobs backed off in surprise.

One thing we're all agreed on is that a defeat is on the cards unless we shape up and fast. Shape up we do, thanks to a back-pass from Phil Jagielka, which Ashley Young latches onto and finishes superbly. Jagielka's one of those players David Moyes has snapped up from the lower divisions and no other managers seem able to find. We used to be experts at that – David Platt being the prime example – but like a lot of other things such as cup runs and shouting Ellis Out every time we go a goal down, it's gone out of fashion.

There's a general feeling that we've got away with it, we should be able to close the game out now that Everton are bound to be destroyed by that breakaway goal. They'll realise it's not their day and accept defeat. Of course, what happened was that Everton piled on the pressure even more, although there was a split-second where the ball managed to escape from our goal area. Villa's defence stood up to the onslaught magnificently, but you just knew what was going to happen. And it did, the equaliser coming deep into injury time. A few of our supporters left at that point, and some of them had probably missed Sidwell's opener. I suppose you can't blame them – we'd come close to getting a win but after being outplayed for so long we couldn't really scream about the injustice of it all.

Cue Ashley Young's solo goal. Cue delirium. The car's still there when we get back, which is always a bonus. We head off through the lights and onto what I fondly anticipated would be a quick and straight road, getting home ahead of everyone else and bringing with us news of Villa's victory to those desperate to hear the result of our journey to uncharted lands. An hour later Percy and the man with the unrememberable name are one more "*It'll be clear once we get past the lights*" away from walking home.

13th December: Bolton (home)

Football's crap once December comes round. It's the law. Bolton the last home game before Christmas tells you what your hardcore support really is, and it's heartening to see what looks like a good crowd turning up. It'll still probably be the lowest league gate of the season, but at least the number of idiotic questions should be less than usual. "*Is that the programme?*" is an old cliché, and one still guaranteed to annoy, particularly when it's asked by anyone wearing a Villa shirt. "*Where's the Holte Stand?*" can be strangely cathartic as you point the questioner in the direction of Witton Station. The best I've ever been asked was one night match against Chelsea. "*Where's Villa Park?*" asked some young idiot, as I stood next to the North Stand car park gates. Thinking this was an attempt at humour, I replied, "*Down there,*" pointing at Witton Island. And off he went on his way.

It's been over a month since we scored at home, and that was in the game we lost to Middlesbrough. We could do with a routine three or four goal win – no more than that, let's not be too greedy – and for the first 15 minutes things look set as Agbonlahor and Young carve open the Bolton defence but find the linesman a bit harder to beat. Then with their first real attack Bolton go a goal up with Elmander backheeling past Friedel. Their handful of supporters get animated for a few seconds. I know it's easy to laugh at Bolton's away following every year and I can remember the times back in the bad old days when we were taking less than this but for a straight trip down the M6 in the customer-friendly 21st century it's pitiful. They're not too upset though, as they're a goal up. Not only that, but they hit the post a couple of minutes later. This definitely isn't going to plan. I remember Bolton have won their last three away games, and it isn't only because it's December that I start shivering. Actually, it is. Does anyone except Scooby Doo really shiver when they think of something bad?

Luckily we responded almost immediately, with Gabby finally staying onside with a classy control and finish to equalise. From then until half-time we played as well as we have for a long time, with Davies being punished for having the temerity to set up Bolton's opener by scoring an own goal to give us the lead. We should have had a penalty as well, when Gary Cahill handled but the referee must have felt sorry for Bolton. And Lee Probert is no name for a ref. You knew where you stood with Jack Taylor and Vic Callow but Lee Probert? He sounds like he should have a Saturday job in Asda.

Half-time is normally spent talking shite and laughing at the Albion score but today the conversation is about how well we're playing. Gabby's looking like he could become world class, Ashley Young already is on this evidence. It's the exact opposite of Chelsea the other week – scored two and could have had six.

The second half isn't as exciting but there's one moment of genius midway through when Young twists, turns and hits the sort of cross that Gabby only has to look at to glance into the net. Ten minutes later it was Agbonlahor who gets the ball on the wing, lays it off to Young and although his shot was deflected that doesn't make the goal any less worthy. Unlike Jasko Jaaskelainen's shirt, which is the brightest thing about the day and draws comparison with Mac's jumpers and Alex Ferguson's nose.

Kevin Davies scored a late goal which was more annoying than anything else. We're fourth now and maybe we should start to think we can stay there.

17th December: (Hamburg away). We never did get to Hamburg. Greg crashed his car last week and couldn't take the replacement out of the country. I should have learned my lesson by now – when making plans involving Greg driving, always factor in the possibility he'll crash his car the week before. Apparently we took loads, everyone had a great time in the markets, bars and gentlemen's relaxation establishments then a below-strength Villa team got taken apart 3-1 with Steve Sidwell getting sent off. My mate Ozz and a bunch of his mates who should all know better flew to Amsterdam then hired a car, all dressed as Father Christmas. Due to a combination of aeroplane difficulties, roadworks and bad map reading they managed to miss the kick-off, and on the way home Ozz's bowels exploded, meaning they had to stop at every services between the German border and Schipol airport. Ozz spent the entire flight home stuck in the plane toilet. Of such experiences are European adventures made. There's a bit of an argument about whether Martin should treat the competition with such scant regard, particularly as so many travelled. There's no right and wrong answer to that one. We'll have to see what the end of the season brings before judging.

20th December: West Ham (home). If I was the paranoid sort I'd imagine the schedulers at Sky and Setenta getting together to see how best they could shaft Aston Villa supporters.

"We sent them to Newcastle on a Monday night two years out of three."

"Well we gave them a 5.15 at West Ham the Saturday before Christmas."

"Nice one, we'll have to see what we can do to beat that."

It's not their fault that we're going down to London today, but it does make matters worse that we won't be back until a lot later than we should. I can never see the point of 5.15 kick-offs. After watching the match the last thing I want to do is see more football, and surely Saturday tea time is the time young people are getting ready to go to those discotheque things they frequent and us oldies are ready to be tucked up in bed. There's obviously an audience although I suspect it's the sort of audience that would watch football no matter what time it was on TV but wouldn't dream of turning up at a match. And they're the ones who take priority.

And so it comes to pass that after two hours in the company first of shoppers headed for the hell on earth that is Bicester Discount Outlet Village and then Home Counties types going Up West I'm standing at Baker Street station waiting, waiting, waiting for a Hammersmith & City line tube to Upton Park. There is, of course, engineering work, what with a football match just up the road the Saturday before Christmas, so an hour later I'm waiting, waiting, waiting at Bow. The train arrives and it's physically impossible to get anyone else on board. Luckily there's one a couple of minutes later so I'm not very late to take up position outside the away end. In fact the turnstiles haven't opened yet and I sell a few H&Vs to the queue. A policeman walks over and to my surprise offers a ten pound note up for a copy. Things have certainly got better. Naturally, I have to play to the gallery and hold the note up to the light. A bit obvious, but it keeps my public happy.

As for the match, it's another one where we're well on top in the first half, Ashley Young hits the post and we could have been a couple of goals up at the break.

We're still not too confident when the team's playing well but hasn't scored and half-time, as ever, was full of how we're going to pay for the misses. As expected, we ran out of ideas in the second half and Carlton Cole did more for us than he ever did when he was on loan at Villa by missing a couple of chances before James Milner's perfectly-placed shot deflected off Lucas Neil and into the back of the net. Of course he meant it. West Ham lost heart after that and we defended our lead comfortably. Sir Graham once described a game at Charlton as "*We came here, we got three points and now we're going home.*" It's been a long time since we were able to get routine away wins – we're either hanging on grimly or, more often than we're given credit for, we put in a stunning display and win three- or four-nil. Hardly ever do we turn up and take three points without hitting top form but without any fuss either. First Liverpool and then Manchester United have built dynasties on such performances.

The final whistle saw a cheer of relief from us, a boo of frustration from the Un'appy 'Ammers and a pleasant stroll back to Upton Park tube, listening to moans all around about "*lucky Norvern Barstads*" and "*that cahnt O'Neill*". The tube's rammed again so I get off at Whitechapel and, guided by the Good Beer Guide, bide my time in a pub at the top of Valance Road, of Kray twins infamy.

That's three away wins in a row, we're now in the top three and set up nicely for the holiday fixtures.

The less said about the train home the better. Did I tell you it was the Saturday before Christmas?

26th December: Arsenal (home). Excuse me while I have another moan about TV schedulers. Football never was the family entertainment it pretended to be back in the days where everyone stood shoulder to shoulder on the packed terraces, pissed in each other's pockets and if anyone swore they were dealt with firmly but fairly by one of the three jovial bobbies on duty. But Boxing Day was a bit different. Your dad would go to his one match of the year and you didn't mind him moaning about how they was all bloody fairies these days and Pongo Waring would have eaten them for breakfast. You could while away the time trying to spot who was wearing their Christmas presents and the stewards would usually turn a blind eye to the hip flasks being passed round. Then it was back home for the Great Escape and an assault on the turkey mountain. Of all the days in the calendar Boxing Day was one for the family and football reflected that. Then Sky and Setanta stuck their oars in.

It wouldn't have been too bad today if it had been an early

kick-off – get the match out of the way by three o'clock and you've got the rest of the day to yourself. Or even a night match – the day at home and go to the match late on. Instead we get the worst of both worlds; you can't do anything before because getting to the match means you've got one eye permanently on the clock and by the time you're away it's too late to go out. Yes, TV brings lots of money into football. Yes, it means the nation will be able to watch us play. But how about, on this one day of the year, putting the supporters first? Wouldn't it be wonderful if the football authorities got together and said that just once a year, if the armchair brigade want to watch a match they can get off their arses and turn up at the ground? Even better, if the can't-get-a-ticket Gloryhunting Reds can't get a ticket to watch a team 200 miles away they should walk down to their local non-league ground and actually contribute to the game instead of taking out. Merry Christmas. Yo ho ho.

Anyway, Martin Laursen's out with, worryingly, a bad knee and Carlos Cuellar takes his place. Arsenal have been, it has to be said, scarily good against us a few times in recent years. Last season's first half drew comparisons with Juventus in 1983 and the Barcelona side of Cruyff and Neeskens. This season they're good but so are we. The difference is that in the first 50 minutes two of their chances go in and six of ours hit the woodwork. Everyone around us is speechless. Well, everyone except The Bloke Behind, who wouldn't be speechless if Cameron Diaz turned up at his house naked. I'm not sure he'd know what to do, but he'd certainly make sure his neighbours knew what was going on.

Then after 64 minutes Gabby was fouled in the box, Gareth Barry scored the resulting penalty and the fight was on. Not only on the pitch – Martin and Arsene Wenger went toe to toe as the match got even more exciting. But it seemed it was going to be another typical second-half Villa v Arsenal – we have the ball, they defend and take the points. Right on the 90 minutes I leave. H&V sales are never particularly good after we've lost but I may as well stand by the bus stop than sit in the traffic. With a bit of luck my over-paid and under-motivated staff will think the same.

I'm just past the Holte when the mother of all roars goes up. We've equalised. Me and the rest of the part-timers who've left early dance around with joy. Some lad in front rings his mate inside the ground and shouts "*Zat Knight???!!!*" More dancing, although he could have said the goal had been scored by Steve Hodge and we'd have been just as happy.

Three years in a row Arsenal have played sublimely in the first half and although we've improved after the break we've been unable to get anything from the match. This season we have. It might only be a point but once more we've rescued a game when all seemed lost, and proved that whatever the opposition, if they're not at their best right up to the final whsitle Villa can match them.

30th December: Hull City (away). Have you got the impression by now that I'm fed up with fixtures being messed around by TV? Here we have another example. What could have been a pleasant Bank Holiday journey to (for me) a new ground becomes a midweek trek for the more dedicated. Once I would have put such setbacks in my stride and either got a lift or spent a few hours sleeping in some railway waiting room. That was in the days when railway stations had proper waiting rooms rather than the draughty bus shelters you get now. And they kick you out once the last train's gone.

My one-man protest extends to not going to re-arranged matches unless there's a good reason, and not watching them on TV either. I don't suppose Sky or Setanta will take much notice, but what if we all did the same? Taking it a step further, what if we boycotted their advertisers? They'd sort things out quicker than Rupert Murdoch changed his nationality, but it will never happen. Too many football supporters have been brainwashed into believing it's for their own good. Sky's been great for the game – look at all the big stars we've got over here now. Oops, sorry, you can't see them because you can't afford a ticket but never mind. Switch the telly on instead. And there's too many of us who think that supporters of other clubs are a lesser breed, serve them Geordie/Scouse/Cockney wankers right if they've got to travel 400 miles on a Wednesday night.

Sometime that evening I was on the phone to Greg. After talking endless reams of shite about Christmas presents and going back to work I remembered Villa were on TV. A few minutes later I flicked over to watch the last couple of minutes. Another last minute winner, another own goal and a bit of controversy over a disallowed penalty. I wasn't all that bothered. Our fourth away win in a row, it took us third in the table and all I can feel is annoyance that I'm not there to watch it. Is it me, or is it football? When in doubt, blame Thatcher. It's been my fallback position since 1979 and I'm too old to change now.

January

It's our year for the cup

2nd January: The transfer window's opened and surely Martin will be able to make a few additions to the smallest squad in the world. It's going to get smaller before it gets bigger though, as Wayne Routledge is moving to QPR. They're about his level, and I can't say I'm fussed about his leaving. I couldn't understand why we signed him and in a few years time he'll be as well-remembered as that Israeli left-back John Gregory signed then never played.

4th January: Gillingham (away). I'd have gone if it was Stockport. But Gillingham's a three hour journey including a trip over the Dartford bridge, which terrifies me. No joke – I hate heights, and bridges a mile or so in the air set me off in a panic. When we drive down to the Eurostar terminals in Kent the panic usually kicks in round about the M1/M25 junction. By the time I can see the bridge I'm almost needing anaesthetic, which is unfortunate as I'm doing the driving. So a combination of idleness, fallinginthethamesfromagreatheightophobia and saving a few quid after Christmas means I'm missing from our band of commandos who set off on the first instalment of this year's great FA Cup adventure. It'll serve me right if I miss out on a ticket for the final. I make do with Five Live, and Sir Graham's expert analysis. This is the sort of occasion he and all traditionalists love. Third division at home to Premier League, crap weather and the chance of an upset.

Villa do their best to be spoilsports by going into the lead early on and it looks like it will be a routine win. Then we fall asleep for an hour and Alan Green's voice rises noticeably as he can see an upset on the cards. Gillingham get a deserved equaliser in that time and his attempts at impartiality go out the window. Ashley Young gets fouled and James Milner's penalty, his second goal of the game, is enough to see us through to round four.

It's been a routine win in the end and Sir Graham hasn't had his upset. Not that he'd have wanted it because despite the clowns who booed him after his final game as manager he remains a Villa man through and through.

It's our year for the cup.

10th January: Albion (home). To reiterate. Albion are our traditional rivals. Their ground is three miles away. They hate us. Now please explain to me the current habit to "*Want Albion to do well*" and "*They're okay with us.*" They're not. One thing I will say, though, is that their supporters are nowhere near as bad as Small Heath's. While our second city rivals arrive at Villa Park (by coach) with a scowl Albion turn up smiling, as though they expect to enjoy getting beat. And they have some good supporters I'm happy to pass the time of day with. Dave Holloway, who runs their travel club and takes my jolly greeting of "*Fuckoffy'dirtysmerrickbastard*" in good part. Terry Wills, guaranteed to be on every phone-in within five minutes of you turning the radio on. And my Goddaughter Kate, whose dad tragically died a few weeks ago after bringing her up singlehandedly to be a credit to him. His funeral was a blue and white affair but a piece of claret and blue ribbon ended up in his grave. He'd have understood. There's also a collection inside the ground for Paul Birch, who's fighting cancer. Former Villa and Albion players are helping out, and it says everything about the respect in which Paul's held that Albion fans are happy to contribute towards a former Villa and Wolves player.

The match starts and there's no Ray Fairfax to abuse. He's in another part of the ground – his mate says the away seats –

which is a pity because he's always good to talk to. We start off well and have a couple of shots cleared off the line before Gareth Barry crosses for Curtis Davies to put us a goal up. Davies refuses to celebrate scoring against his former team, one of those bits of sportsmanship which have crept into the game recently. I wouldn't have any time for that myself. If I scored against the Albion I'd run around the pitch laughing in the faces of every one of their players and most of their supporters as well. In fact I'd find every photograph of the goal, get hold of the Albion mailing list and post copies to everyone on it.

From then on we were even more in control, Gabby and Steve Sidwell both missed chances, then came one of the highlights of this or any other year. Gabby hits either an inaccurate shot or a harmless pass far too near to Scott Carson. However, to the great delight of all, and especially me, Carson scoops the ball over the line. It's another blow to the keeper's confidence and at any other time I'd feel sorry for him. He's obviously talented but he's going through the bad patch all keepers endure at some stage. Some of them – Peter Shilton being the best example – come out of it better for the experience. Some of them don't. Whatever happened to Richard Wright?

We should have run up another Small Heath last season scoreline, but three minutes before half-time we let them back in with a daft goal. The second half is a bit of a worry as well, as their less-than-incisive midfield dominated possession a bit too easily for my liking. The World's Greatest And Most Put-Upon Supporters Ever were enjoying themselves, singing hymns and suchlike while all around me in the North Stand Upper was wondering what was going on. I hope Martin was as well, because Albion are crap yet were on top for most of the second half. Luckily their training sessions must comprise of sideways passing four days a week and an hour making excuses on Friday morning, because they seemed incapable of getting the ball into our box.

As the fourth official holds up his board I nip out to get to my usual after-match selling spot only to find the North Stand gate locked. The police have pulled their own Small Heath last season trick of a barrier across Witton Lane, only this time they haven't bothered to tell anyone. Why they do it today, God knows. Albion supporters are a different breed to the other lot over the city and the rivalry, such as it is, never borders on hostility. The organised hooligans will find somewhere miles away to fight and the ordinary supporters aren't interested. All this over the top security does is inconvenience fans and make us resentful of the police. I double back through the North Stand car park, run up Trinity Road, hearing an anguished cry of relief as I pass the Holte and get to Sales Pitch 1 seconds after the final whistle. There's the usual business done here, a few words of joy exchanged with regulars and once the crowds have died down I go back to where my car... isn't.

A couple of phone calls later I find it's been towed away by orders of the police, who wanted my space to put up one of their totally unnecessary barriers. Fair does, it wasn't exactly legally parked but whatever happened to tannoy messages of "*Will the owner of vehicle registration number....*"? Who cares about good relations when you can make a couple of hundred quid? Welcome to Rip-off Britain. I eventually find out where it's been taken. Mac, God bless him, drives me over there and we negotiate with the car-jackers to get back their booty. In normal circumstances it would be called extortion but this is football and normal doesn't apply.

At first the thieves won't let me have my property back until Monday because "*the pound shuts at one on Saturdays.*" The car wasn't brought in until three, but that's no matter. It can be opened to store stolen property (sorry to labour the point but I didn't want them to take it yet they did. In my book that's theft) although not to retrieve their contraband. At this point I make a couple more calls, and the thieves become surprisingly more amenable, to the point where they ring one of their bosses who's only too happy to come and let me have my car back. For an extortionate fee, and they try to make out they're doing me a favour ("*I'm only doing it 'cos you're a Villa fan like me.*" If you were a Villa fan you'd have been at the match instead of stealing from your own), but at least I've got it. The calls I made were to my solicitor and a senior police officer, while my press card was visible in my wallet at the time, but I'm sure this was merely a coincidence.

By another coincidence, but this time the sort that makes the world a happier place, I'm meeting a couple of Albion fans tonight, including the aforementioned Terry Wills. Bless his heart, he's in a better mood than I am. I suppose that when you're an Albion supporter the Premier League is still full of magic and wonder, so who am I to disillusion him?

17th January: Sunderland (away). The excuses for not going to the match just keep rolling in. I know – last Saturday's unexpected expense has to be clawed back somehow. That'll do.

Martin Laursen is still out and the ever-unreliable Carlos Cuellar continues in his place. Maybe that's unfair, but for the money he cost Carlos should have shown more so far. There was a time when giving 100% was enough to be appreciated, but for me those days went when £1,000,000 stopped being a major transfer fee and became a reserve's annual wage. When you cost as much as Carlos Cuellar did and you get paid his wages maximum effort and an ability to do the job without excuse should be the very least we expect. There's been a tendency in recent years to explain away the poor form of new signings by saying they need time to settle in. Try changing jobs in the real world and see how much settling-in time you get. A day or two, maybe a couple of weeks if you're lucky. Stilyan Petrov got two years, and although he's playing well now he still owes us.

I'm chewing this over while watching a Midland Combination game in a field near Solihull. The crowd is outnumbered by the players and almost gets less when one of the subs breaks off from warming up on the other side of the pitch to tell one of the crowd (if you can call 17 a crowd) that the referee's had a word and if he keeps arguing with the other team he's going to get booked. The spectator that is, not the sub. Whenever I think football's vanishing up its own arse I watch a non-league game and remind myself that the game's great, it's just the people at the top who ruin it.

It's a two o'clock kick-off so the end of the match here is half-time at the Stadium of Light. We're a goal down and fortunate it's only one. Time for mystical forces to come into play. I spend an hour avoiding any mention of the game and at five to five switch on WM to find that despite Ashley Young being sent off we've won two-one.

The stewards at Sunderland are notoriously 'efficient' and one or two of our supporters might have been warned but I doubt the referee has threatened to book anyone.

21st January: I'm sitting at home putting the final touches to the next H&V when I get a message that Johnny Dixon's died. This is a bit of a shock; I knew he wasn't well but hadn't expected it to be this sudden. The last time I'd seen Johnny was in August 2007 at the banquet to commemorate amongst other things the 50th anniversary of the FA Cup win. Johnny entered the room holding a replica of the trophy with Peter McParland and brought the house down. He deserved nothing less.

22nd January: Just as I'm walking into the Central Library I get a text that begins "*We regret to announce the death of...*" I think it must be a repeat of one from yesterday but I look again and it's Vic Crowe. Although Vic was a bit younger than Johnny his death was less of a surprise as he'd been suffering from Alzheimer's for several years. It's surely no coincidence that so many former players suffer from this disease and I can't help pondering that a week's wages from every player in the Premier League would work wonders in helping find a cure. As it is, the PFA and organisations such as the Villa Former Players

Association do sterling work in whatever way they can.

23rd January: A text from an unattributable but reliable source tells me the signing of Emile Heskey is imminent. If I were a civil servant I'd call the deal 'interesting', or possibly 'brave'. Time will tell.

24th January: (Doncaster away). Another cup tie, another away draw and get this – Mr Part-timer is going. This one takes us to a new ground, the ludicrously-named Keepmoat Stadium at Doncaster. Last time we were up here it was the old Belle Vue for a League Cup match that ended in the humiliation of a 3-0 defeat on the worst night of O'Leary's reign, and that's saying something. As with most new grounds this one is one the edge of town and dangerously close to a shopping centre, which means my dear lady wife is taking an unnaturally close interest in the day's proceedings. She says she doesn't mind whether I take her up there or not, which as the world and his dog knows is woman-talk for I've got a passenger. She can pay half the petrol in that case.

When we get there you can tell they're not used to big crowds; there's no fluorescent-clad security men checking number plates or signs warning of dire penalties for anyone parked longer than a couple of hours. Rich arrives and we begin a tour of the man-shops – KFC, check. Pub, check – before heading round to the away turnstiles to peddle unofficial literature. I'm doing a decent trade when my assistant comes round to tell me a head steward has stopped him from selling and threatened him with arrest into the bargain. It's his ground (well, in his own mind it is) so he can do whatever he wants. I carry on selling with Rich doing a stoic job as lookout. The steward who stopped him walked past a couple of times while I stood there looking innocent and definitely not breaking any ground regulations by selling anything unauthorised on club property.

Opinion on our new signing is surprisingly positive. Most are of the opinion that he's improved a lot in the last couple of years, and definitely in the past 24 hours, and everyone agrees he has to be given a chance. It says a lot about Martin that almost three years into the job he can sign Emile Heskey to near-unanimous approval. What would have happened if O'Clueless had done the unveiling I dread to think.

Inside, the ground was much as expected. The Keepmoat is another bland, featureless new ground, bigger than Walsall and smaller than Bolton. The match featured a struggling Championship team who were up for it and a successful Premier League team who weren't. We had more or less a full strength team playing but there was something missing. That's the modern FA Cup for you. A couple of chances were saved by veteran keeper Neil Sullivan while Doncaster hit the post twice. Meanwhile, my young assistant spent a chunk of half-time being waved at by two policemen. When they finally attracted his attention, PC Hamilton and his colleague wanted nothing in particular except, we later reckoned, the chance to inconvenience an innocent member of the public.

Two minutes to go and I commit the cardinal in many eyes sin of leaving early with the scores level. It's winding down for 0-0 and I've got bad memories of trying to leave this sort of ground by car. As I leave I walk past the steward from earlier, who is issuing instructions to a couple of his colleagues. Another hour and his moment of power will be over for another fortnight so he's making the most of it. With a lighting (!) turn of speed I'm back at the car more or less as stoppage time begins, to find my travelling companion drinking possibly the first cappuccino ever sold in Doncaster after having done her bit to kick-start the South Yorkshire economy.

An old and quite frankly pathetic superstition means I refuse to listen to the radio until our match is definitely over. Five Live takes an age to get to the Keepmoat, where I find that as predicted I missed nothing in the last couple of minutes and we've got a replay. We're home just after seven. "*How come you take longer than this to get back from Villa Park?*" I'm asked, quite unreasonably in my view. "*They play more stoppage time in the Premier League,*" is the reply. "*Something to do with the tickets costing more.*"

I never did get her share of the petrol.

27th January: Portsmouth (away). The debut of a new signing always causes excitement, particularly when it's a current England striker. At least I assume it does, because when was the last time we signed a current England striker? Not this century, nor for a huge part of the last one.

If this was a weekend game I might be tempted to head south, but it's Tuesday and I don't fancy the drive back late at night (excuse for missing matches no. 78 of the season). To think I once stayed four hours at Reading station after a midweek match at Southampton where Steve Hodge made his debut.

It's the radio again, and this amazing new invention called DAB. I don't know what it is or how it works but it means you can listen to all sorts of stations you can't get on a proper wireless. One of them's called Five Live Extra, and that's who's doing the commentary. Even better, there's no egotistical presenters or ex-players chipping in their words of wisdom. And to make things perfect they're commentating on another Villa win. Emile 'the predator' Heskey has scored on his debut and no matter how much of the ball Portsmouth have they can't get past our rock-like defence. Belhadj gets away with a vicious assault on the mild-mannered Craig Gardner and gets sent off later on, while Peter Crouch does us a favour by recalling his time at Villa and missing a gilt-edged opportunity for an equaliser.

Crouch is a confusing character. When he was at Villa anyone with sense could see his promise yet he got dog's abuse for some reason, probably because he was signed by Sir Graham, who was appointed by Doug and therefore an Ellis stooge. It didn't help that he was also seen as in competition with St Juan Pablo the Blessed, a player who could do no wrong and for whom all excuses shall be made. Yet even Crouch's biggest fan would never have predicted that he would end up being transferred for several small fortunes and become an England regular. Anyone who said he and Emile Heskey would be the first choice striker partnership of England manager Fabio Capello would have had all sharp instruments taken away from them and given a very wide berth thereafter.

But the highlight of the evening wasn't the score, or even Heksey's goal. It came when the commentators on the radio were discussing Villa's sponsors. "*Do you know what that Acorns on the shirt is? It's a local children's hospice. Villa have given them their shirt sponsorship.*"

"*Yes. There's something about the Villa that makes you feel the club are doing things right.*"

31st January: Wigan (home). No-one has ever been able to explain why Villa crowds and the associated sales of fanzines and assorted merchandise shoot up after Christmas. Maybe it's the psychological effect of surviving the festive season – you've spent all your money on everyone else and you've got a couple of quid left over. Anyway, we do as many as we did on the first match back in August and I'm happy on behalf of my sales force.

Before the game I get word that Paul Birch isn't expected to last the weekend. I knew he was in a bad way, but it's still a shock to hear confirmation. Tribute was paid to Johnny Dixon and Vic Crowe, in the form of a minute's applause. I'm not keen on that – clapping isn't difficult but keeping silent and reflecting for a while takes a bit of thought. But the decision isn't down to me and if the men's families were happy then the rest of us have no cause for complaint.

The first half was no great tribute, as uneventful as we've had this season. After half-time Villa improved and Wigan keeper Chris Kirkland had to be on top form as we had a pile of chances. John Carew, back after injury, missed a couple and even Zat Knight got into the act with a shot that hit the post. With twenty minutes to go Mac turns to me and says "*One of those days.*" He's right, although we can but hope right until the end. Top clubs don't have one of those days, or if they do it's once a season at most. We seem to have them every month. It's ever more obvious that if you want a point from Villa Park and you do the simple things without making any daft mistakes, chances are you'll get one. Close mark, don't let our lightning-quick forwards get in front of your defenders and you'll be safe.

The final whistle goes but the match had ended long before then. It's another two points dropped and they're all starting to become important. Three of the top four are starting to get their acts together and Arsenal will surely do the same soon. We've got to take advantage while we can and that includes beating Wigan at home.

February

Retreat from Moscow

2nd February: Paul died in the early hours of Monday morning. Naturally, being Birchy, he had to battle a bit longer than anyone expected but even he couldn't win this last one. I'm looking at messageboards from the clubs he played for and they all say the same thing – he gave his all in every match, whether it was Villa against Inter or Halesowen in the Southern League. The Aston Villa Celestial XI have had a few new recruits recently and they don't need any more for a while.

4th February: Doncaster (home). Of course the away team are bringing loads, and it's the law that within five minutes of pitching up at Villa Park I see the only Doncaster fan I've ever known, John Coyle, who's an out of town gloryhunter from Solihull I first met in my FSA days. We have a quick chat which ends up costing him £1.50.

It's a good job Donny are making a big thing of the game because our turnout is poor. I remember our cup run in 1980 (it was our year to win the trophy then as well) when we got 43,000 odd for a fourth round replay with Cambridge, who were in the second division, then the round later Blackburn, of the third, pulled in even more. If we get half that many tonight we'll be doing well. It's another sign of how low the FA Cup ranks in the perception of the modern football supporter. For all the talk about respecting our heritage, they're still only interested in the Premier League.

There's a well-respected minute's silence for Birchy before

the game and the 90 that followed weren't much louder. I'm in the Witton Lane downstairs so I can't see how many Doncaster have brought, but there's a few of them in the North Stand upper. I hope they enjoy the view.

Seven changes to the team who played Wigan, with the cavalry in the shape of Gareth Barry and Gabby Agbonlahor on the bench. I can understand Gabby – with half an hour to go he could get us out of any mess we might have dug ourselves into - but Barry will never change a game like this. The best news is that John Carew's starting for the first time in three months and he wastes no time in putting himself around a bit, setting up a goal for Steve Sidwell and hitting a 25 yarder that looped off a defender and into the net.

Two up inside 20 minutes and it could be a night to remember, then we sit back and Doncaster snatch a goal on half-time. They come out for the second half looking to cause an upset but their reputation is well-founded. Lots of nice passing but nothing to show for it. On the hour Nickey Shorey's cross is headed home by Nathan Delfouneso. It's a first senior goal for the Fonz, as he's bound to be known to the delight of tabloid sub-editors, and that's the match wrapped up. Former Villa player and husband of local singer Jamelia, Darren Byfield, comes on for Rovers. There's a bit of applause but a lot of the crowd were hardly out of nappies when he was playing for us. The attendance is a disappointing 24,203, and it would be fair to say the away fans made up the odd 4,203. One day Sky will have to answer for their crimes against football and destroying the FA Cup will be right up near the top of the charge sheet.

Full time, and while once more the fringe players – Gardner, Salifou and Sidwell for example – have scarcely advanced their cause we're in the fifth round, which is all that matters.

It's still our year for the cup.

7th February: Blackburn (away). I came up here by mini-bus to a cup tie in 1990. We parked up and were met by a police inspector who, rather than telling us what we couldn't do under threat of arrest as was the norm in those days, pointed out a couple of away-friendly pubs, the best chippy and told us to ask one of his officers if we wanted to know anything. Gobsmacked by this early example of positive policing, we proceeded to set fire to the pubs, destroy the ground and embark on an orgy of violence not seen in the mill towns since the Spinning Jenny riots of the 1830s. I'm lying – everyone was perfectly well behaved and so began a tradition of the Blackburn Drinkathon which continues to this day.

I've arranged to pick Rich up from where he's exiled in the quaint Lancashire village of Ramsbottom. It's possibly the most Northern place in the world – pie shops and cobbled streets abound. On to our destination, and the pub we've been using for a few years. Right off the motorway, a couple of miles from the ground but at the wrong side of Ewood Park so it'd take serious tracking down to find. The only problem is a landlord who's a law unto himself when it comes to opening and at well past 12 there's no sign of doors being unlocked so it's plan B – follow the Good Beer Guide to an alternative on t'moors. Middle of nowhere but a massive car park bodes well. I can imagine that come summer this place would be rammed out but it's the beginning of February so there's just us two, a couple of ramblers and a dog to share some highly drinkable beer.

It's another pub that takes some leaving, but with a promise to ourselves that we'll be back next season we're off, parked and soon standing outside the ground. Bitter experience has told me that despite the friendliness of the place, you can't sell on the club's land at the back of the away turnstiles. It wouldn't kill them to turn a blind eye, but they never have. Steve Whitehouse in his Holy Trinity days was once told to stop leaning against a wall. Anyway, we start selling on the pavement outside, only to be informed that the club own the road and we can't sell there either. Fortunately, the order is given by someone who soon has to do some proper work and we carry on regardless.

There's been a lot of noise coming from the direction of the Fernhurst, as expected, and at just after half past two comes the inevitable news that it's gone off in there. Nobody knows what or why, but the pub's been closed and we endure that truest of cliches, the drunken minority who spoil it for everyone. A couple of them are either too pissed or too stupid to realise there's only ever one winner when you argue with a policeman at a football match and get themselves arrested. An anonymous candidate for Wanker of the Season puts a bottle under a coach wheel – the team coach. I know we all did daft things when we were younger but I don't want to be around when the reason for that one's being explained.

Blackburn were unbeaten in nine matches but that record was never going to last much longer. Emile Heskey, God bless him, was running round looking like the powerhouse England international forward he is and could have scored a couple before James Milner's goal in the 22nd minute. Just the one before half-time although Gabby had another disallowed, and the interval singalong downstairs is long and loud. There was a time when it was better than the football and a few of our choristers didn't bother returning to their seats, but everyone was back to see the start of the second half. Ashley Young and James Milner continued to carve the home defence apart and the only fault was that we should have scored a lot more goals. It took until the last couple of minutes for Gabby to score with a deflected shot, but that was the only drawback of the afternoon. That and a second candidate for Wanker of the Season, seen happily smashing a toilet after the game. I hope he gets dysentery and can't find one. The rest of us are singing about Manchester United like we're their rivals and maybe we are. The way things are going this run could last until May.

Rich suggests jogging back to the car to get out a bit quicker. I give him a puzzled look. How long has this man been my friend? And he still asks stupid questions? There's a bit of a delay but not much and we're soon on our way. The pub we wanted to go in before the game is still closed or maybe it's opened then shut again.

Later on that night I'm watching Match of the Day and it's been a long, long time since I heard anyone talking so positively about the Villa. Emile Heskey is the bargain of the transfer window and we're not just improving, we're there to stay is the general consensus. I've always said Alan Hansen talks a lot of sense.

8th February: Small Heath Asda (neutral venue). It's not me being biased, that lot are definitely different to us and never more so than when we're all supposedly off-duty. I can think of nothing dafter than a grown man wearing a football shirt to do the shopping but they consider it their sacred duty to wear replica shirts and managers jackets in all weathers. A few weeks ago in the checkout queue I heard a man say "*What's that in German?*" to a child who couldn't have been any older than eight. The kid spoke a few words of fluent German, then did the same in French. He was wearing a Villa kit. Today I look at a specimen of humanity with a shaven head and the words 'Trust no bitch' tattooed across his throat. On the side of his neck was the globe and football mark of the underclass.

They're different to us.

10th–13th February: Belgium. With no football and work slack there's no finer place to spend a few days than a country built on chocolate and beer. We spend part of Friday afternoon in a bar close to the Eurostar terminal in Brussels and I raise a glass to Birchy, whose funeral is taking place around that time.

14th February: Back home and catching up with the arguments online. As always before a cup tie there's a big row going on between the traditionalists who still think football's about winning trophies and an unholy alliance of the new breed who believe in the doctrine of Premier League uber Alles plus those who say that whatever Martin does is fine by them. In pointing out that nobody remembers the massive success of finishing fourth I get told I can't see the bigger picture by an American who had never heard of Aston Villa until Randy took us over. That's me put in my place. I also catch up on what's been said about us this week, and it's quite scary. *"I'm not surprised Villa are in a good position because they've got some good players,"* says Rafa Benitez. *"They've done absolutely magnificent,"* is the slightly ungrammatical opinion of David Platt, who normally never has a good word for us. Newcastle managing director Derek Llambias says *"We aim to be like Aston Villa."* Paul Jewell chips in with *"Villa are a bigger club than Chelsea."* Meanwhile Karren Brady's saying *"I never dun nuffink"* to the rozzers again. Her and her boss must have answered more questions than a Mastermind finalist, but with more passes.

15th February: Everton (away). After all the arguing I never did get there. Some old injury flared up and my foot was, to use a medical term, bastard well painful. Driving would have been too dangerous and even by train the thought of walking around then standing for two hours was too much to bear. At least I hadn't gone to the trouble of getting a ticket – it isn't giving away too many trade secrets to reveal that for a Sunday on TV there's always spares available. Someone's mate is working, or skint, or got so pissed last night he missed the coach, or one of a hundred other reasons, and they've got a ticket to offload. I'd normally take the gamble and go without a second thought but today I am the Ivo Stas of our travelling support.

I watch a bit on the telly, I listen to the radio, I go online. Whatever the medium, the story's the same. Everton are up for it and go ahead after three minutes. Even when we equalise through a Milner penalty it was never going to be our day. They get a pen of their own after 24 minutes and although we had a couple of chances their third goal in the dying minutes killed off the game.

Tell me how the league's the only thing that matters and you won't be any help although you might get an earful of abuse for your trouble. 52 years. Don't anyone tell me the FA Cup isn't important anymore.

18th February: CSKA Moscow (home). There's a TV presenter standing in the middle of Witton Lane, being filmed. Not only are simpletons waving at the cameras, they're ringing their friends to tell them they've just been on TV. Not one of them has recognised the European Cup winner being interviewed, and this at a club where Failing to Acknowledge the Boys of '82 was one of Doug's gravest crimes. It was Andy Blair, fact fans.

A 7 o'clock kick-off, which is a new one even for us, and from the North Stand we can yet again see that CSKA have brought a decent number of noisy and colourful supporters. Yet again it's what's been called our Channel Five select XI, and as has often happened over the years we make a slow start against a European team we've not heard much of. Inter, Barcelona, Ajax – into them from the kick-off. Banik Ostrava or Celta Vigo get a goal start. Mac, Percy and I look at each other with the air of three who have seen it all before and the inevitable away goal is scored by Wagner Love, who will probably be linked with a move to us for the next ten years.

It wakes the team up a bit and they start to play well, Ashley Young in particular causing all sorts of problems on the wing. John Carew eventually equalised with a header in the 70th minute but rather than step up a gear we seem content with the draw. As ever after a night match there's a horrible, horrible traffic queue but at least we get to the Barton's before ten for the in-depth post-mortem. There's one good thing about weird kick-offs.

21st February: Chelsea (home). If we have to be on TV 12.45 on Saturday is about the best option. At least it gets the match out of the way and you can start enjoying the rest of the day early. One thing I do notice is the amount of tourists around the ground. I'm all for attracting new support and we all went to our first game once, but there's something deeply wrong about the sight of Japanese tourists posing for photos on Witton Lane.

Gus Hiddink has taken over at Chelsea and as he emerges from the players tunnel there's the expected scrum of photographers. One of these days they'll be taking photos of our manager or something we do. I know both Martin and Randy like to do things calmly, professionally and above all quietly, but I sometimes wish that just for once it was Villa in the news. Then again, remembering news like Paul Merson's assorted addictions, Mark Bosnich's stag night and the 24-hour rolling news story that was Stan Collymore, perhaps we're better off leaving things as they are.

Anyway, this is the biggest test since we started looking like title contenders and to put it mildly, we blew it. Anelka got their only goal but they were a yard sharper than us. As the unusually-astute Rich said, "*There's as much difference between us and them as there was between us and Blackburn.*" Considering there was 12 places between us and Blackburn and there are two between us and Chelsea, it tells you as much about the Premier League as you need to know.

Half-time is the usual summit meeting about what we're doing wrong and how we should put it right, but there's not a great deal that can be said. We aren't doing anything particularly wrong, we're just not as good as Chelsea. The top four clubs are different to the rest of us; all they have to do when they play even a best of the rest side like Villa is the basics. Get them right, avoid too many mistakes and they'll win.

The team improve a bit in the second half and both Gareth Barry and Gabby have good chances saved. I've noticed how I hardly mention Barry in match reports this season. Is that because he's not playing well, or because he gets on with his job without making a fuss? I'd like to think it's the second, but there's something about him that makes me wonder. When he first came into the team all those years ago (he was signed on the day Brian Little resigned and made his first team debut two months later at the ripe old age of 17) Barry was as good as any player I'd ever seen at that age – Gary Shaw, Gordon Cowans, Little himself. But he'll never be a legend like they are. Barry's good when we're playing well. When Villa are on top he'll be hitting thirty yard passes and making surging runs all day. In a match like this, when we need something a bit out of the ordinary, he's not there.

Are we really good enough? It's not long since we were talked of as outside contenders for the title. Maybe that was pushing it too far but we've lost three matches in a week. Out of one cup, probably out of another and finishing in the top four's looking harder. This is where Martin starts to earn his wages.

23rd February: The squad is announced for the return trip to Moscow and the howls of anguish can be heard echoing around Birmingham. To call it under-strength hardly comes close.

26th February: CSKA Moscow (away). If I didn't go to Everton I was hardly likely to go to this one. Steve Whitehouse flew over and managed to miss the kick-off, which is good going and he should be congratulated for it. Missing the game altogether would have been easy, getting there days in advance a piece of piss, but to cut it so fine you're getting off the underground when the game kicks off is genius. The team Martin put out did themselves proud but they just weren't good enough. They managed to hold out until the second half, but once CSKA scored they were the only team who were going to hit the back of the net again, even if it did take them until stoppage time. Whisper it gently, but having a few quid on CSKA to win might not have been a bad idea. There, that's my treasonable thought over for the season.

That's also our hopes of winning a trophy gone. The debate will rage on, but Martin's taken a gamble and he's the one who'll have to take the blame if he loses. One thing's for certain – if we don't beat Stoke on Sunday the temperature will go up several degrees even if it is only the beginning of March.

March

The wheels are falling off

1st March: Stoke City (home). Yet again the Stoke internet goodwill mission has been in full blast this week, with their supporters wishing us a good afternoon and please tell them they'll stay up.

Standing on my corner over the years you can always tell what the away fans are going to be like. Some are an amiable bunch – Sunderland for one. Others are horrible. For an hour or so Stoke are great. Loads of family-type groups enjoying their season in the Premier League and delighted they're doing well. I talk to a few of them about players who've been at both clubs, policing and the best places to drink near the ground, the sort of things supporters all over the country have in common. They're good people and I'm feeling well-disposed to them. The half-hour before kick-off sees the dregs arriving. Stoke are one of those clubs who built up a hooligan reputation by terrorising supporters in the lower divisions once hooliganism was out of fashion and it appears they want to do the same here. The police are out in force, ushering them into the ground. I've never seen a team have two such different types of fans.

We're still fourth, five points ahead of Arsenal, four behind Chelsea and Liverpool. A win this afternoon and we'll have forgotten all about the cups with the Champions League still in our own hands. The match itself started off promisingly enough. Luke Young was getting to the byeline and putting crosses over, even if they weren't causing much danger. Stoke, as expected, were concentrating on defence and it looked as though they would be level at half-time when a shot from Stilyan Petrov on the edge of the area seemed to have Thomas Sorenson unsighted and we were a goal up. Thomas Sorenson not seeing a shot that went in – who'd have thought that?

Sorensen must have been affected more than we thought by the goal because he didn't come out for the second half. His replacement, the confusingly similar-sounding Steve Simonsen was busy after the break with a few crosses that were banged up to Emile Heksey, with little effect. Then Heskey came off with an ankle injury and was replaced by John Carew, who picked up a pass from Petrov and swept the ball over the keeper's head from 25 yards out. Not bad for a target man with not much skill, or so some would say.

That, surely, was it. Stoke have offered nothing except a couple of runs from substitute Ricardo Fuller and with long-thrower Rory Delap out they've got no attacking threat at all. We took a bit of time to break them down but that's because they're defending in numbers rather than anything to their credit. They might not be Swindon in 1993 or Derby last season but they are truly dreadful. How did they beat us last August? How have they beaten anyone? Why aren't we six up by now?

With three minutes to go we're still trying to work this one out when Shawcross beats the lumbering Zat Knight to a cross that just goes over the bar. Villa have noticeably switched off and that should be a warning. But no – seconds later the same thing happens. Beattie cross, Knight nowhere, Shawcross header. The only difference is that this header's on target and Stoke, unbelievably, have pulled a goal back. It's a consolation, it must be. They've not been in our box all game and here they are pushing for an equaliser. Ninety minutes are up, surely we can hold on now. This is what we conceded the UEFA Cup tie for, so we wouldn't be knackered in the next game.

There's a new H&V out today so, reluctantly (!) I've got to draw myself away from the game and get up to Mac's bus stop to sell afterwards. That and talk incessently about how we shouldn't be desperately holding on against Stoke. As I walk past the Holte I hear from behind the sort of cheer starting at the corner of the Witton Lane stand that you know can only mean one thing but you hope you're mistaken. Seconds later comes the confirmation that Stoke have equalised, and seconds after that the final whistle. Our supporters are naturally pissed off while the Stoke ones I see are going on about taking four points off us, as if that's all they're bothered about. Maybe we're turning into the Manchester United of the Midlands – even the clubs we don't care about see us as their rivals. It might be a compliment but it's certainly not a consolation.

Two points dropped, but the effects could go a lot deeper. This week has seen Martin's first real criticism since he arrived. If we'd won the Moscow debacle would have been forgotten. Now it's bound to get worse. With some tricky games to come March could prove to be a long month.

4th March: Manchester City (away). Anyone remember the Platt Lane stand at Maine Road? It held about ten thousand, and there were rows of wooden benches nobody ever sat on. You never stood on the floor either – Platt Lane was strictly for standing on the benches and it's a miracle nobody got hurt. There I go with my double standards. It was alright to play about when I were a lad, but the youth of today should bloody well behave itself.

Anyway, we've braved the M6 and the Mancunian rush hour. We've found a car park which is both safe and easy to get away from. We've even found a pub that's not too far from the ground but not too football-orientated so it doesn't come with this membership fee rip-off. One of these days I'm going to get knocked back at a pub because it's "*Members only lads, sorry*" and demand to see the membership list and club rules. I'm sure there's some licensing loophole to exploit there.

As usual we get chatting to some locals and as usual Percy's innate Brummieness takes over. I'm the opposite – five minutes talking to anyone and I'm picking up their accent, but Percy invariably retreats into the Jim-Baines-voice-coached-by-Ozzy-Osbourne style that makes Carl Chinn sound like a Fab FM presenter. Put him in a pub a hundred miles away and he'd drink Bacardi Breezer if you told him it was bottled at Aston Manor. It's always easy to get on with Manchester City supporters; there's a mutual hatred they're only too happy to share. In truth, they always seem a bit too happy to find out how much you hate their Stretford neighbours. City are a big club with traditions, yet a lot of their fans spend more of their time talking about United than their own team. Maybe it's a blue thing.

They're getting excited at the prospect of their new owners buying them every good player in the world but as Miles Barter, ex-Radio WM presenter and founder member of the Handsworth Wood Manchester City Supporters Club (membership: one), said recently, "*All the new people who've just got into football think we're going to do well. But anybody who knows anything about City knows we'll find a way to fuck it up.*"

We walk down to Eastlands and very impressive it looks with the lights on. Not a proper football ground of course, but you can't have everything. It's the same team as Sunday, which means Carlos Cuellar retains his place at right-back. I suppose it's nice to see Martin being loyal but we spent two years waiting to buy a right-back then he gets shifted onto the left side while we still have a makeshift on the right. We've got Heskey and Agbonlahor again up front with three forwards on the bench. That could make things interesting.

As the game kicks off I look round at the travelling support and think how much we've all spent in terms of money, overtime payments, swapping shifts, favours owed and family harmony disrupted. The least we can expect is a good performance.

And what we get is a half-hearted, tired looking display that belies the fact we've won our last seven away games in the league. Shaun Wright-Phillips was quite frankly a pain in the arse. He ran down our left wing, then he ran down the right and when he got tired of that he ran through the middle. He hit the post, had another shot saved and finally got brought down by James Milner with Elano scoring from the spot.

We improved a bit after the interval and Shay Given had to make a couple of good saves. But Brad Friedel was a lot busier and the inevitable second goal from City came after Stephen Ireland, who's good enough to play for us, laid the ball off to Wright-Bastard-Phillips to curl round the keeper.

It wasn't that far back to the car and we did manage to get out and away quickly but that's about all you could say of the evening. Six matches without a win, that's not good. Footie fans are supposed to listen to 6.06 on their way home after the game, for the banter and discussion. We got the Booker T box set. Listening to the extended version of Time Is Tight is a much better way of getting over a defeat than Tim Lovejoy going on about pens and linos and Stevie G.

5th March: The team are off on a training break to Dubai. I know this might be a good idea; warm weather training, team bonding, away from the pressures and all that, but footballers jetting off to the sun while the season is falling apart isn't very tactful.

15th March: Spurs (home). Spurs at home has always been a bumper gate and a big game feel, but there's none of that before the match today. Sell-out or not, the feeling of pre-match optimism is missing for the first time in a couple of years. Maybe it's the Sunday kick-off, or maybe that's what a few setbacks have done. You could write a book about the mindset at Villa; we never seem to have any confidence or big-time swagger. When we're in a big game we never behave as though we belong, when we're doing well we don't expect it to last. This means every minor setback is seen as a return to the natural state of affairs rather than a temporary blip and that's what's happening today. Before the game I talk to Pat Murphy of Five Live, who calls it the biggest game of the season and he's not far wrong. If we don't win this one we can say goodbye to the Champions League. Arsenal are back on form, they've overtaken us on goal difference and our next two games are away at Anfield and Old Trafford. A month ago we would have been confident of getting something from at least one of them but now I fear it will be back to our old damage limitation mentality.

Curtis Davies has been dropped and Carlos Cuellar takes his place in the middle with Nigel Reo Coker at right-back. It didn't make much difference as we went a goal down after five minutes when Brad Friedel couldn't hold a cross and Jermaine Jenas reacted quicker than our defenders to poke the ball home. It was another one of those goals where nobody was totally at fault but equally nobody was able to do anything right. Friedel maybe should have held onto the ball, Reo Coker and Knight could have reacted quicker. Over the years we've been spoilt as all our successful sides have been built from the back but now it seems we have to give an avoidable goal away almost every game.

From then on things improve. Ashley Young is storming down the left wing, tying Didier Zakora up so much that he gets substituted after half an hour with his boots on the wrong feet. When he's on form like this Ashley isn't far off all-time great status, but either the final ball isn't there or our twin strikers are having a joint off-day. That's not entirely fair – Emile Heskey headed against the bar in injury time. "*That would have gone in a month ago*" was the general consensus.

Four minutes after half-time Wilson Palacios shoots, Friedel pushes the ball out and Robbie Keane's ball into the box is forced over the line by Darren Bent. An ex-Blue and our nemesis are involved in the goal. It figures.

And now comes the sequence of events that months later, I'm still trying to understand. Zat Knight is replaced by John Carew. Nigel Reo Coker moves into the centre and then left-back, with Luke Young in the middle and James Milner our latest right-back. With me so far?

This makes no difference so Nathan Delfouneso replaces Gabriel Agbonlahor. As Gabby leaves the pitch there's a distinct but not too loud cheer from the crowd. Whether it's relief because Martin has made a substitution that doesn't take a physics degree to work out, or because our latest bright hope has arrived into the action, I'm not sure. Then with eight minutes to go Emile is brought off to be replaced by midfielder Craig Gardner.

It makes no odds, we still don't look like getting anything from a game that's drifting towards its unsavoury conclusion. Then with five minutes to go James Milner's cross is headed home by Carew. But even when the goal goes in there's no roar of encouragement to the team in the hope they can get an equaliser. Everyone seems to have accepted defeat. As I overheard after the match, "*By the time we play at home again we could be six points behind Arsenal.*" Wild pessimism, surely – things can't be that bad.

Martin has a go at the supporters who were booing, saying "*That was no way to treat him.*" He thinks it was Gabby who was being booed, I'm still not sure. It won't make things any better whatever the reason.

20th March: Martin seems to be warming to a theme, criticising "*The new found Villa fan that we have, who obviously wasn't supporting the side a couple of years ago, has turned up now and has decided that winning supposedly mediocre games in the Premiership is a fait accompli.*" I do hope he's not turning into David O'Leary.

22nd March: Liverpool (away). I know plenty of decent Liverpool supporters and contrary to myth they're employed, own their own hubcaps and don't rob anyone, least of all their own grannies. All that thieving Scouser/You'll Never Work Again stuff is boring and about as accurate as the Thick Brummie stereotypes we've put up with for decades. Most of the pubs you go into around the ground (if you can get into them) are friendly and the only problem is annoying Devonian/Welsh/ Scandinavian types going on about how the Magnificent Reds will come again and vanquish the heathens from Manchester. You even get them, with no trace of either irony or a Scouse accent, talking disparagingly about gloryhunters. It's like the Sioux and the Ghost Dance they thought would drive away the white man and bring back the buffalo to the plains. I don't know whether they're more annoying than that Reclaim the Kop lot who want to Keep Anfield Scouse. The party's been over for about 20 years lads, all that's left is the Tesco lager and even the ugly birds have been taken.

Park, pay (no point in trying for a free space here), find pub we've been drinking in since Sir Graham was first in charge. Pub's closed so we end up in some poky little place where either the smoking ban doesn't apply or it's going to take at least three more years to get rid of the accumulated fug from decades of lung abuse. I hate smoking but this is my sort of pub, if a bit too popular at the moment. The paranoia that comes from having spent your formative years travelling to football matches in the eighties kicks in and we hardly say a word but everyone knows we're Villa supporters. Don't get me wrong, there's no threats and nothing made me feel in any sort of danger but we didn't belong. The whole of Liverpool has that ability. You can't get lost in a crowd there, you always stand out. So we make our excuses and leave, getting into the ground earlier than I have for many years.

Normally I'd be peddling offensive literature outside, but there's no point at Liverpool. Not only as for some reason we don't sell much up here, but stewards and police combine to cause grief. We've been told not to stand by the turnstiles, forced to stand on the opposite pavement and had one of our sellers arrested at the FA Cup quarter final in 1992. That wasn't long after a policeman showed me a knife he'd taken from a Liverpool fan but hadn't bothered arresting him – obviously wanting to stab someone is less important in the eyes of the Merseyside Constabulary than selling fanzines.

So we spend a pleasant almost an hour watching the ground fill up. There's no doubting Anfield's sense of occasion. It might be a routine league game but this is the kind of atmosphere you only get at somewhere like the Bernabeau – and Old Trafford tries ever so hard to repeat. You'll Never Walk Alone is the ultimate football song, although Dave Chance might disagree. We had a bit of a debate on our website and in H&V about when Villa stopped singing Walk On, but nobody really knew. It was one of those things – one minute it's there, the next it's gone. There's a minute's silence for the Liverpool club secretary who dies last week, and it's good to hear nothing, if you know what I mean. Not that I expected our fans to be anything but immaculately behaved, but the trouble with silences is that one wanker can get national coverage

Liverpool are slap bang in form at the moment. In the last couple of weeks they've scored eight goals against those no-hopers Manchester United and Real Madrid while we've forgotten what a win looks like. Naturally we're convinced there's going to be an upset, but that hope takes all of seven minutes to extinguish. Liverpool hit the bar, our defence can't clear the ball just for a change and it's one-nil.

We didn't play too badly after that, with Reina having to make a couple of good saves from John Carew as we piled the ball into Liverpool's box at every opportunity. Then just as we start thinking we might get an equaliser, Reina launches a clearance that – are you ready for this – our defence can't clear – told you it was a surprise – and we're two down. God knows what's going on with our back four. As long as I can remember they've been the cornerstone of the team but lately they can't do the simple things, like marking at set-pieces and clearing loose balls. I don't spend too much time on that particular puzzle because we've soon given away a penalty as Nigel Reo-Coker, again at right-back, has brought down Riera. Steven Gerrard steps up and you know what's going to happen next. Three nil.

There's the usual half-time inquest and the verdict is that we aren't playing too badly, it's just one of those things. We've missed our chances, they've scored theirs. It happens, especially when you're out of form and the opposition are on a roll.

Back out for the second half and no sooner have we settled into our seats, or rather into the space in front of our seats than there's another goal. Stevie Bloody Gee scores, and you know what's going to lead the sports news for the rest of the day. Does he like being called Stevie Gee? Has anyone told him it makes him sound like an eighties tribute singer? Then he finishes off his hat-trick with another penalty after Brad Fridel brings down Torres, getting sent off for good measure.

A few of our supporters start drifting out at this point while the rest of us stay to the bitter end defying the odds and expecting to win 6-5. Liverpool have given up, saving their resources for the harder battles to come. The final whistle blows and everyone hurries home. They're not particularly bothered about beating Only Aston Vila while I for one just want to be away and forget about it all.

We got beaten, heavily, and we were in a perverse way lucky. Seven or eight-nil, the sort of score you never forget, looked on the cards at one stage. Were Liverpool that good, or are we really this bad?

We have plenty of time to debate the issue in the traffic home. At one point, after moving a hundred yards in ten minutes we pull up alongside a car full of Liverpool supporters. Super Reds stickers all over his back window, gesturing passengers and his side window's down. Percy does likewise. "*Going out tonight mate?*" he enquires. "*Dunno mate, why?*" comes the reply. "*If you are can you get me an ipod and a DVD player?*" asks our very own Jasper Carrott as the lights change and we hurtle away after scoring quite possibly the only claret and blue victory of the afternoon.

April

We'll win again...

5th April: Manchester United (away). Another one I refuse to go to. Actually, it's not another one it's just about the only Premier League ground I won't attend on principle, under any circumstances. I can't stand their philosophy but although someone else will take the ticket (and if they don't Manchester United will hardly miss forty-odd quid) I feel that somehow I'm making a stand against the greed and globalisation of modern football. They've got a patched-up team which nevertheless has a bench full of internationals and stars of the future. If we had as many players missing Martin and John Robertson would start with Paul Faulkner on the bench.

I'm watching on some internet feed while tapping away at a computer but it's like listening to the radio in the days of Sports Report on Radio Two as United go a goal up inside 13 minutes. Thoughts naturally go back two weeks but it doesn't take long for them to be forgotten. Today Villa do indeed stand up to be counted and first give as good as they get, then begin to dominate. The equaliser comes on the half-hour as makeshift central defender Gary Neville is outjumped by John Carew, whose header rockets into the back of the net.

Neville gets shifted to full-back, where he's pulled apart by Gabby and Ashley. Half-time and no further goals. This is when you'd expect Sir Alex to pull some tactical masterstroke, but they really have got nothing to offer. Villa come out for the second half supremely confident and it's no surprise when Agbonlahor puts us 2-1 up after 58 minutes. He's one for the big occasion, Gabby. For years we've had a succession of players, especially forwards, who go missing when they're needed but here's one who seems to thrive on pressure.

This afternoon I've gone from writing and looking occasionally at what's happening on the screen to having one eye permanently on the match. Now I've given up trying to write as I'm staring at the images in front of me. For a second I think it must be one of those YouTube mock-ups but no, Villa really are winning at Old Trafford. Not only that but we're looking good for a goal that would not only give us the three points but also, just maybe, hand the title over to, er, Liverpool.

This is the time when they usually bring on Rooney, or Tevez, or maybe Giggs, but instead Fergie's last cigarette is some kid out of the reserves. With Nigel Reo Coker on for the knackered James Milner our attacking threat is less and United start to take advantage. Ten minutes of normal time to go when Ronaldo shows what a great player he is, the bastard. I've now given up watching. I go out of the room, walk around the garden, anything to avoid having to listen to the final, inevitably heartbreaking, minutes of the match. And when I do switch on the radio I can hear Daz Hale sounding genuinely upset while BFR is talking about how well we played, much good it did us.

Naturally thoughts turn to that game against Sheffield Wednesday in 1993 when United kick-started a faltering title challenge with two late goals after the ref allowed for more injuries than they had at Gallipoli. I'm not normally one for conspiracy theories but you do wonder whether Mike Riley would have been so generous if Macheda had scored in the last seconds of normal time.

Normally I wouldn't listen to 606 if we'd lost at Old Trafford because hordes of gloating Cockneys and Devonians would have me slinging the radio through the window. Tonight I still don't.

7th April: Tonight's the night of the Moscow meal, when those who went to see the reserves in the UEFA Cup get a slap-up feast in the Holte Suite, complete with lashings of ginger beer no doubt. The cynic in me wonders how much it will cost Aston Villa FC to put on a meal in premises owned by Aston Villa FC, with catering by Aston Villa FC and bar takings going to Aston Villa FC. But as ever, they didn't have to do it and it's a nice gesture. Beforehand a few press people want to know what might be going on, but it's all off the record and that should be respected.

12th April: Everton (home). The idea that we could be six points behind Arsenal by kick-off time was, as predicted, wildly inaccurate. They've already won so the gap is now nine points and surely we've blown our chance of the Champions League even though Percy is trying to tell me all the way from Stechford to Aston that they'll blow up.

Once more we seem to be inundated with tourists, and some of them even have their photos taken with friendly British bobbies. What's going on here? Have these people never heard of the West Midlands Serious Crimes Squad? Don't they know armed robbery is a serious offence and they could get 14 years? Longer if they're guilty. Even worse, how will the police react? For years they've cultivated this image of the Villa Park constabulary as on a par with the French CRS and now they're smiling with tourists. Next thing you know Doug will be standing on Trinity Road handing out ice creams to children.

Everton supporters love to make themselves out as a cut above, and every coach that arrives you expect to be full of Versace-clad models parading along Witton Lane sipping lattes. It's a bit of a disappointment when they're on the whole a load of replica shirt and baseball-wearing little rats singing the same songs everyone else sings and looking for de away pub la'.

On arrival at the ground, with my usual appalling lack of punctuality, I look around the pitch and what's this I see? It's Nicky Shorey at left-back and Luke Young on the opposite wing. This idea of playing players in their proper positions will never catch on.

With us fifth and Everton a place behind but catching up fast neither team want to lose and the first part of the match is therefore quiet. Nobody wants to make the mistake that will leave their side chasing the game but it's Everton who go a goal up after 20 minutes thanks to a long ball, some slack marking just for a change and a tap-in for Fellaini, who's certainly boosted Everton's season since he's started playing further up front. Four minutes later and we're two down. It used to be us who were deadly at corners. Now it seems there's panic every time the ball comes near our box.

The second goal finally reminds Villa there's a match going on, with Young and Milner doing well on the wings and firing in crosses for John Carew. After 33 minutes he gets on the end of one that finishes up in the back of the net. When he's on form Carew is as good as any centre-forward in Europe. Realistically, if he was on form more often he wouldn't be with us, so we may as well enjoy it while it lasts, one way or the other.

Half-time comes and there's the usual mixture of nonsense spoken (Mac, Rich and me) and wise insight courtesy of just about everyone else. Then the football starts again and we're treated to yet more excitement although unfortunately it's at the wrong end. Pienaar finishes off a sweeping move with a classy 20-yard shot that beats Friedel, the sort you can't help but applaud even though it's probably finished our season.

But no, two minutes later Milner scores an even better goal, a free-kick that smashes past Tim Howard from 25 yards out and we're back in it. Two minutes later Stilyan Petrov is judged to have been held back by Joleon 'Villa Fan' Lescott, Gareth Bary gets his fifth penalty of the season and we're more than back in it.

Maybe both teams then realised that not losing was more important than trying to win, or more possibly it's been a long season and they were all feeling the pace. The game begins to wind down just when it was getting very exciting and although substitute Nathan Delfouneso looked lively, full time comes with a 3-3 draw that did neither team any good but both would probably have settled for at the start. It's been a cracking match which fully deserves the ovation at the final whistle.

It's that great dilemma, a point saved or two dropped? It almost certainly means we'll be finishing sixth and while such an exalted position two seasons in a row is nothing to be scoffed at I can't help wondering whether we'll look back at this season being our biggest wasted opportunity since we were one player short and Brian Little signed Stan Collymore.

The usual selling afterwards, complete with a post-mortem or twelve, and back we head down Witton Lane as the coaches full of supporters of the Proper Liverpudlian Club begin their journey home to such Merseyside suburbs as Rhyl and Chester. It's the first time I've parked in this spot since the Great Automobile Robbery against Albion so it was a bit of a relief to get back to find the car still there. Two minutes later I'm standing in the middle of the road exchanging insurance details. There I was pulling onto the main road when somebody decides to reverse and not bother looking in his mirror or wondering why that horn sound seems to be getting nearer. Jinxed. It's the only word.

18th April: West Ham (home). If it always seems to rain against Portsmouth, the weather's usually good against West Ham. That's one of the reasons there's always a decent crowd and despite our poor form there's almost forty thousand inside Villa Park again to witness out latest must-win. The 1966 World Champions have recovered after a poor start to the season. They're seventh now and although they can't catch us, please God, they'll still be a handful for a team who are starting to look like they want the season to end right this minute. I usually regard every other player from every other team with an opinion ranging from apathy to deep hatred, but Gianfranco Zola was one of those players you couldn't but admire. I'm glad he's turning into a good manager.

As ever I get into the ground at ten past kick-off, exchanging words with the smiley and totally barmy girl on the late turnstile and the friendly steward downstairs. As I climb up the last flight of stairs I hear the familiair "*Gooaaaaaahhh...yessss!!!!*" that means I've missed a goal and can nip into my seat while everyone's still standing up without getting in the way. Apparently Emile Heskey has bundled the ball over the line after James Milner set the chance up. I'm not too worried about missing it – I'd rather miss one of ours than see one of the opposition's.

It seems like I'd be able to see plenty more as we battered West Ham for the rest of the half. Milner, Ashley Young and Heskey all missed stone-cert opportunities to make the elusive three points certain and do our goal difference some good. I was enjoying it so much I forgot myself and waited until half-time to nip downstairs to the toilets. Villa Park might be the most wonderful place in the world to watch football but don't go downstairs in the North Stand if you're in the slightest bit worried about being in a confined space. Get as many sweaty blokes in as small a space as possible and turn the heating up. You might after an hour or two have some idea of what it's like in the North Stand concourse at half-time. Eventually I fight my way to the toilet and strike up a conversation with a perfect stranger. This is the only situation where the previous sentence can be written without George Michael or the Metropolitan Police becoming interested, and we agree that Villa are playing well but need another goal.

We had a couple of chances but West Ham gradually got back into the game and for the last twenty minutes our goal was well and truly under siege. We looked like we might hold out but with five minutes to go Diego Tristan got hold of a shot that was going nowhere and stuck it in the onion bag. Has anyone ever used the expression 'onion bag' apart from 606/Soccer AM types 'ironically' (A word that belongs with 'banter' in Football Hell)? Even then Brad Friedel had to pull a header from under his bar, although being Villa we had a good shout for a penalty right at the end, or the death if you're a feature writer. The only worry at half-time was whether our inability to score more than once might cost us. In the end thank God West Ham didn't equalise any earlier or they might have got three points. We'll win again, don't know where, don't know when.

24th April: Our house (depends). *"Darling husband...... how far's the Trafford Centre from Bolton?"*

25th April: Bolton (away). Once again I had no chance. Drop my good lady wife off, then go back in time thirty years to pick up Rich. Pub, park, start selling. A steward comes over and asks what we're up to. I tell him and mention that we're always okay with the Villa security main men. "*Fuck the Villa security*" he says, pleasantly. Nice man. But we have no other interference, and carry on selling until the teams come out.

The view at Pride Park, sorry the Madjeski, er we're in the north so it must be the JJB no hang on, yes that's it, the Reebok, is very nice but unfortunately it shows too much of Bolton attacking in the early stages. As often happens in such situations, the not out of relegation trouble yet home team soon run short of inspiration and we have a good spell before half-time which culminates in Ashley Young's cross being missed by everyone and ending up in the back of the net.

We could have scored another couple, but after an hour came the inevitable defensive cock-up that lead to an equaliser. Yes, they do still have that stupid flag waving and fanfare when they score. Gavin McCann, a hard-working pro who epitomises the good side of football and Jlloyd Samuel, a waster who's just the reverse, are as desperate to win against their old employers as you'd imagine but although we have a few hairy moments it's a draw, which probably suits Bolton better than it does us.

I'd managed to find a crafty parking space before the game and even better, got away straight on the whistle so I was off while everyone else was attempting to get away from the Black Hole that is the Bolton matchday parking experience.

Unfortunately, while I might be the sniffing-out-a-parking-space equivalent of Paul McGrath I'm also as accurate at finding directions as Tony Daley was with crosses. I take a wrong turning and end up close to the old Burnden Park, which is ironic considering how hard it was to find when they played there, before I'm able to turn round and as a result get mixed up with all those annoying football supporters. The much better half is waiting to be picked up with several bags full of spending her way out of the recession and hasn't noticed I'm an hour late. Not for the first time I wonder why the Greater Manchester conurbation has a network of motorways that could stretch to the moon while we have to make to with the Aston Expressway and Hagley Road.

27th April: Albion reserves (home). Tony Butler's finally retiring. At least twenty years too late, but he's leaving WM at last. No more of his xenophobic ravings, no more harking back to the good old days. It's a pity he went on too long – there's an entire generation who think of him as an embarrassment rather than the most innovative sports broadcaster in the country. Further evidence that I've sold out to the establishment comes with this evening's entertainment, seen from the comfort of the posh seats courtesy of Paul Faulkner. Mac and Paul's colleague talk computers while I'm almost certainly an embarrassment to our host with my regular and impassioned pleas to avenge Alex Cropley. Albion traditionally take these games seriously, doubly so against us, and I've known them field almost a full first team when our reserves have been the opposition. Tonight's not that bad and despite playing beneath themselves Villa are coasting to the win that will give them the reserve southern section title thanks to a first-half goal from Nathan Albrighton, when we spy Tony Mowbray leaving. He gets a friendly "*cheerio*" and misses James Collins' stoppage-time winner that makes the title certain. Yet again the future's in good hands.

May

Sob on the Tyne

4th May: Hull (home). When the news broke that this one had been shifted there was an internet furore that registered high on the Richter scale of such happenings. As you might have gathered by now I'm not too happy when matches get shifted anyway, usually for the very selfish and mercenary reason that fanzine sales are never as high as for Saturday afternoons. But anyone with a modicum of sense would realise that moving a game from Saturday to Bank Holiday Monday evening, at three weeks notice, is going to cause serious inconvenience. Not least to Hull supporters, who would have otherwise sold out their allocation.

Villa have done the best they can with this potential PR disaster, having a bit of a family day with promotional stuff on the Trinity Road concourse. It's not their fault, but the fact is that all the Premier League clubs happily and greedily sign up to the TV deals every time they're due for renewal and to my knowledge not once has one of them said "*What about the supporters?*" Guilt by association is still guilt.

I'm happily peddling my wares on Witton Lane when two notable incidents occur. First, a question even dafter than "*Where's Villa Park?*" An elderly Hull fan asks me how long we've been playing at Villa Park. Since 1897, I reply. "*Oh, I've been here before then,*" is her answer. Words fail.

Next up I hear a Scouse accent from behind. Normally this would be a sign to check your pockets but it's the familiar voice and even more familiar face of Dennis Mortimer, who used to be a regular on Witton Lane but now arrives on the other side of the ground. We chat for a few minutes, well he talks and I agree with everything he says, and as ever hardly anyone notices they're walking past the greatest Villa captain since the Victorian age. As stated earlier (I always like to make a point at least a dozen times when I'm building up a good head of steam) this is something that particularly pisses me off. One of the most regular moans when the anti-Ellis campaigning was at its height was the lack of recognition given to the stars of 1982. It was a justifiable complaint as the way they were ignored for years was a disgrace. However, and this is a regular occurrence, they never seem to be noticed anymore. I might be doing a disservice, but it strikes me that they were a useful stick to beat Doug with.

There was a football match as well. Hull are even worse off than us at the moment and played like it. Nothing much happened for over half an hour then George 'Legend' Boateng lost the ball to Stilyan Petrov, who set up an attack that John Carew finished. Nothing much happened afterwards either, although our former youth keeper Boaz Myhill won man of the match with a string of good saves. Maybe we should have kept him, but a young keeper is never going to get any better stuck in the reserves and has any of them ever broke through at the club where they first started? No, I can't remember either.

Not a game to remember but it's a win at last, and that'll do for now.

9th May: Fulham (away). If Blackburn is the most popular away trip for throwing as much down your throat as is humanly possible, Fulham is the alternative for those who prefer a more civilised approach. As it's London there's plenty to do in the way of pre-match entertainment, even if it does come at a price, and a delightful walk along the Thames before arriving at the charming Craven Cottage. That's the Sarah Beeney bit over with, now onto the game.

I'm meeting Barry, who's had to come from the centre of London while I've made a hundred mile journey so naturally I'm at Putney Bridge tube before him. A short walk past the Eight Bells, always the pre-match haunt of those who head for the first pub and don't stop to think it might be easier to get served somewhere else, then over the bridge itself to the Bricklayer's, which is out of the way enough to be used to football supporters without getting too rammed out. There's a few Villa fans in there, paying the West London prices without too much choking, and it's a pleasant afternoon to sit out in what passes for their beer garden. I wonder how much the land is worth and calculate the room provided for each table would buy a small house in a normal town.

I'd like to stay here a bit longer, but this is Fulham and there's no pub good enough to keep me away from the paying public. It was a few years ago we discovered that games in London attract a different breed of Villa supporter to other aways and this type is happy to spend money. Barry and I while away a hectic 90 minutes parting them with their £1.50s and striking a happy (for us) compromise between standing where we want to sell and where the police want us. Then at a few minutes after kick-off, with the stragglers finally having had enough £4 pints, I'm inside the ground and that's where the fun stops.

There's only six minutes gone before a couple of sharp passes carve open our ponderous, porous defence and James Milner has to resort to bringing down Kamara in the box. The penalty that puts Fulham a goal up seemed to wake the team and it's not long before Ashley Young prods home Milner's cross to put us level. Then Ashley hits the post and although we're level and doing well, there's an ominous feeling about the way the players left the pitch at half-time.

I spend a fair chunk of the interval looking around the 'neutral' section of Craven Cottage. It's mostly Villa supporters and I suppose that if you've brought your kids it's a good idea to have them sitting in an area where the atmosphere's a bit, well, diluted is probably the best word to describe it. What the tourists this area was originally intended for make of it I don't know but I'd like to see their faces if they fancy watching another match in London and Millwall are the only team at home.

Someone timed Fulham's second goal at 26 seconds after the re-start. Diomansy Camera got it, as he did their third, from a corner. Brede Haageland had been a nuisance to us all afternoon and he went up the other end to lay on the goal for Camera, who flicked the ball over the line with his back to goal. Big defenders coming up for set-pieces and causing havoc; that's what we used to do.

There's still half an hour to go but the ref might as well blow the whistle on this game and our season now. The players are going through the motions and even our supporters have stopped trying to encourage them. Their over-exuberance might get knocked sometimes but our fans on their travels rival the best and if they're not bothered it just shows how things have changed in the past three months. Emile Heskey comes on and it looks like Martin has a row with Nickey Shorey as our left-back is being substituted, but that's about all the excitement for the day. There have been worse performances but it's been a long time since I saw a Villa team who seemed so disinterested. I hope it's because they know the season's almost over and they're looking forward to a fortnight in Weston.

For the first time I'm starting to hear serious mutterings about Martin O'Neill's ability to improve on where we are. "*Taken us as far as he can*" is a phrase I usually think is nonsense – after all, if a manager's taken you that far nobody can tell whether or not he can take you any further because logic dictates that neither you nor he have been there. But in this case I'm starting to wonder. This isn't Scotland, nor is it the Premier League of Martin's time at Leicester. To improve on top six he'll have to bring in the sort of players he's never managed before.

If you don't hang around at the final whistle you can usually beat the crowds back to Putney Bridge. Even better, I take the gamble of walking back to the High Road and jump on a bus. Normally when I get a bus on the off-chance in London it's going to Brixton, or Heathrow, but this one's perfect. If you want to go to Earl's Court, that is, and you don't mind sitting in a traffic jam for half an hour.

By the time I get to Earl's Court tube there's no point in trying to beat anything. The tubes will be full and the train home the same. I find a pub and two minutes later I'm in a conversation with a holidaying American who wants to find live music. Some elderly bloke joins in with the story about how Jimi Hendrix used to live down the road and sit up that corner there when he wasn't hell-raising. The old bloke used to bring his guitar along and they used to jam together some nights. Even the American doesn't believe him, but he's harmless enough.

After a pleasant hour talking about the relative music scenes in New York and Birmingham (I lied a lot) I'm on my way. It's hard getting a seat on the train at Marylebone, there's two women on a table and a polite "*Excuse me, is this seat taken?*" forces them to begrudgingly move their bags and let me sit down. I get a few stares but they're off at High Wycombe and I have the table to myself from then on. Of such simple pleasures are life's joys made.

16th May: Middlesbrough (away). Every time a supporter whose knowledge of football goes further back than Euro 96 makes a comparison between then and now you can guarantee they'll include something about Middlesbrough. It never had the reputation of Millwall or Leeds, but going to Ayresome Park in the old days was as bad as it got. I well remember the second division season of 1987-88 when we were allowed out straight after the game but kept in a holding area just outside the away end. Normally you'd be looking at ways of nipping past the police escort to make a quick escape or engage in what's now called banter with the home fans. Not here. The collection that wandered past us looked like a scene from an eighteenth century painting – Convicts Arriving at Van Diemen's Land, or similar. They never said a word, neither did we. They didn't have to and we didn't want to.

Then Steve Gibson arrived and ushered in a new era. New ground, lots of new players, not much success and a lot of new supporters. Disneyland came to town, Boro's a safe place to visit and we usually go home with three points rather than a smashed windscreen.

One of Gibson's traits is an admirable but flawed sense of loyalty to managers. Bryan Robson was kept on long after the time when everyone else could see he'd replaced Bobby Charlton as the most obvious example of how a great player doesn't make a good manager and even though Boro are certs to go down Gareth Southgate is under no real pressure. I can never understand why Southgate gets so much stick from Villa supporters. He gave us great service and only said what many were thinking. By the time he left he'd fallen so far out with John Gregory that he had to leave and for some unknown reason they were the only club who came in with a firm offer. I'm not saying he didn't get a hefty pay rise out of it, but to say money was the only reason for his move was wide of the mark.

But that was then, this is now, and if Southgate loses his job because Boro are relegated after we've beaten them six-nil this afternoon I'll shed no tears. I don't mind driving to Boro; the train's unfeasibly expensive and every coach I know is leaving way too early with drinking on their mind. Percy's come up trumps again having persuaded a couple of his drinking buddies to tag along and share the petrol money so I get the opportunity to witness the sun rising over Chelmsley. It's the last away game of the season, which was once an excuse for drunkenness and mayhem on a grand scale but things are a bit quieter these days. Instead it's fancy dress, with much expense and imagination having gone into some of the costumes. Percy's come as a scruffy bloke from Birmingham while to be honest, I could be mistaken for a catwalk model en route from Milan. Provided they're in a show modelling this year's collection from the House of Sports Division (three quid t-shirt selection).

We're in a pub on the outskirts of Middlesbrough town centre. I can't remember the name but I know it did decent beer. Talk turns to new signings and I'm trying to persuade the assembled throng than I know no more than they do. Or less, in one case; "*We're in for David Bentley. Spurs want £12 million and we're offering ten. We'll be paying him forty grand a week.*" I never cease to be amazed how many football supporters suddenly become so well-connected when the transfer window approaches. Everyone knows someone who knows someone who knows an estate agent/hairdresser/steward at the training ground and has the inside track on what's occurring.

The ground's not far away and we stroll towards it with hopes high. After all, this is Middlesbrough and we've got a good record here. Even news that James Milner is something like our eighth right-back of the season can't dampen the optimism.

Then we kicked off, and after ten minutes even Percy was starting to complain. "*This is a bit crap,*" was the spot-on analysis of Chelmsley's Happiest Man as we watched Villa second to every ball and getting the run-around from a team in even worse form that we are. The inevitable goal came after 14 minutes when Tuncay got hold of a ball that was flying around and hit an overhead kick that Brad Friedel could only watch as it sailed into the back of the net. Credit where it's due, it was the sort of goal you'd normally associate with a player like Marco van Basten, or possibly Doug Ellis. Boro fans celebrate, which they're entitled to do, but not with the Great Escape theme. That sort of idiocy should have died out with Sheffield Wednesday ten years ago.

Twenty minutes gone and Boro winger Stewart Downing, who's been a right pain in the arse to us so far, comes off second in a collision with Stilyan 'The Enforcer' Petrov and has to be carried off. You don't like to see opposition players injured, with the possible exception of Robbie Savage, but he'll do more good for us in the treatment room than on the wing.

Half-time sees the usual discussions. A couple of bananas

reckon we're good bets to go down next season if we carry on like this. King Kong says if they keep talking like that he'll eat them.

The second half is a different kettle of bananas entirely. Middlesbrough have clearly blown themselves out and we're on top. Gareth Barry gets the ball, the home defence can't clear it (where have you read that this season?) and there's John Carew to equalise. It's been a long time since we've had a number 9 like Carew – Dion Dublin for a few months, and before that maybe all the way back to Peter Withe. No matter what formations and tactics might be in favour, there's nothing like a big target man to get the crowd behind him.

We could have scored a couple more but don't, and although a draw is a bit of a disappointment given our second-half performance it's a lot worse for Boro. Their supporters boo the team off the pitch, which is understandable, but while they're now down barring a miracle at least there don't seem to be much of the tears before bedtime that usually accompany relegation. I like Gareth Southgate and I always thought he would make a good manager but should he get the sack – you have to wonder how long Steve Gibson's loyalty-over-reason can last – he couldn't be blamed for counting his pay-off and settling for an easy career with his old team-mate Andy Townsend on TV. The bananas are now saying Martin's a genius and they're putting money on us getting into the Champions League next season. We're not kept in and there's no human gorillas chasing us back to the car.

24th May: Newcastle (home). The season reaches its climax this afternoon with what Sky is calling Survival Sunday, and I wonder what marketing genius got paid thousands to think up that piece of alliterative genius. The players spend the morning wandering round the grounds of their hotel, maybe having some light training and a final team talk. I spend the countdown to kick-off walking round Small Heath Asda. I stop to look at the papers – it is annoying when you want to buy one and someone's in the way, I know – and the front of the Mercury has a story about a "*Blues player in gang link*". There's a surprise, and I turn the page to see they have an interview with Mark Ward, ex-habitue of the criminal element and later prisoner. Next to his story they run photos of Zak Knight and Darius Vassell, both of whom were "*Villa players linked to gangs.*" Naturally there's no mention of them in the story, even more naturally there's no evidence of such links. You have to hand it to the Mercury. Any excuse to throw dirt at the Villa and they'll grab it with both hands.

Driving to the ground I'm surprised at the amount of Villa supporters already queuing for the number eleven, but then again the weather's warm so it's the first time since September they've been able to wear shirts and nowt else.

By the time we get to the ground there's a load of Newcastle in evidence and the talk is of 20,000 coming down. Apparently that's what Stan Collymore said on Talksport, and he should know shouldn't he? Always had his finger on the pulse, has Stan. On the planet the rest of us inhabit realism kicks in. If loads of the Toon Army were expected to descend upon the second city ticketless, police would be checking coaches as far back as Hartlepool. That sort of thing just doesn't happen these days and Collymore should be a bit more responsible than to say it. All such comments do is let some meatheads get excited.

There seems more away fans than normal around, but that's probably once more down to the weather, with Newcastle fans showing off those back and white stripes unencumbered. There's no real problems outside the ground, a few Newcastle young idiots are shouting but that's par for the course. One of their older fans asks where he can get a programme and I reply "*Inside this week. Next year you'll get them at Doncaster.*" For a moment I was proud of my rapier wit, but he took it in such spirit that I felt a bit ashamed. For a second.

Scunthorpe have been promoted to the Championship after

beating Millwall at Wembley. With Leeds and MK Scabs also in the play-offs Scunthorpe have been in the unique position of being the most popular club in the country for the past week. It's nice to see the good guys wearing claret and blue. Let's hope we can keep it up.

As usual I missed the kick-off, and the first few minutes. En route to my seat I stopped at one of the refreshment kiosks for a drink but all they had was ordinary Coke, the one in the middle of the North Stand was a bit better-stocked and relieved me of £1.60 for a bottle of water. Villa Park might be one of the cheapest grounds in the league to get into, but the benevolence ends once you go through the turnstiles.

I've missed a couple of Newcastle attacks and it becomes apparent that I've missed all their threat for the game. If you'd asked anyone before kick-off what the match would be like they'd have predicted a frenetic, 100mph, all guns blazing assault from the visitors but they just don't care. Their supporters made a lot of noise at the start, particularly when the news came over that Hull were a goal down to Manchester United reserves, but they soon became engulfed in the apathy their team were displaying.

Villa weren't much better, but at least we were showing some attacking promise. Maybe not in the 33rd minute, when Gareth Barry hit a shot with little power and hardly more sense of direction, but the ball hit Damien Duff and crept inside the post to give us the lead. You felt that if anything would stir the Newcastle team into action that would, but no. The rest of the first half went by in a blaze of apathy, both teams performing as though they were already on holiday.

Half time saw a decent gesture, as family members of the former players who have died during the season were presented on the pitch and we have a minute's appreciation while their photos are displayed on the big screens. Paul Birch naturally gets the biggest reaction but it's good to hear the applause getting noticeably louder when Vic Crowe's picture comes up.

The second half continued much as the first half ended. We passed the ball around without much urgency, Newcastle showed hardly any appetite to get it off us. Maybe their players did think their careers would be best served by relegation. Michael Owen came on midway through the half and the stage was set for the perfect TV script, but he hardly got a kick. Four minutes of stoppage time and Mac nudges me. "*Look where the cameramen are,*" he says and they have, indeed, moved en masse in front of the away section to capture the reactions of the 'emotional' Newcastle fans at the final whistle. Maybe they're on a bonus – so much for tears, a bit more if the Toon Crier they film is topless and the jackpot if he has "*We'll be back*" tattooed across his exposed gut.

There's no goalkeeper joining the attack in the dying seconds, no hit-and-hope desperation that served Manchester United so well That Night in Barcelona. The only bit of excitement comes when David Edgar clatters into Ashley Young, it's his second booking so he's allowed to miss a ending that has looked inevitable for half an hour. Never has a one goal lead been so comfortable in such circumstances.

All afternoon there's been a banner draped over the top of the Holte saying "*Who's your next messiah – Ant or Dec?*" The design and colour give away the author as Leighton Castle, whose previous works have included the seminal "*We're not fickle, we just don't like you*" aimed at David O'Leary. As whatever danger there might have been is cleared, today's effort is joined by another, larger effort saying "*Sob on the Tyne.*" Leighton again. He should claim for image rights.

Seconds later comes the final whistle and Villa supporters celebrate wildly. Why does everyone dislike Newcastle? I suppose it's because the media make so much of them, but that's not their fault. We moan that we don't get enough coverage; would we object, therefore, if our training sessions were broadcast live and our star striker sneezing made headline news? Of course not, but we're heading into the realms of rational thinking now and God help all of us if football supporters started thinking rationally.

Outside the ground there's a few police on Witton Lane and some Sky Sports cameras interviewing Newcastle fans. Nothing could better show how football's changed – by rights supporters who've just got relegated should reposition the cameras where the cameramen can't see them but these days people will do anything to get on the telly.

A final settle-up with my last couple of sellers and a "*Where are you?*" phone call from Rich, who in fairness I'd forgotten I'd arranged to pick up, and we're away. Rich tells us there's been a few fisticuffs on Witton Lane and some bricks thrown at the coach park. Compared to the scenes when we relegated Coventry eight years ago it was nothing, in keeping with the low-key nature of the day.

And that was that for another season. There was a time when the last game was inevitably accompanied by a mad all-day drinking session (home) or a trip to the seaside (away – even if we were playing Coventry) but life's not like that anymore. My generation is too old for such silliness and the Sky generation haven't been told to do it so they don't.

It's at times like this that you look back at the previous nine months with fond memories and look forward to what the summer will bring. We finished sixth again, which by modern Villa standards is highly commendable consistency. We gave the teams above us a real scare and for most of the season looked like we might finish fourth or even higher. For the first time in years we have players who any club in the country would want, should they become available, and even more surprisingly they're not for sale. But against all this good news has to be balanced the fact that for the last three months of the season we were poor. Martin showed signs that he might not be infallible after all, and the first mutterings of discontent could be heard. This will be a big summer, but we've come so far in the past three years I don't want to believe we'll stop now.

Postscript:

24th June: It's now a month since the season ended. Gareth Barry, after all he spouted about the Champions League, was off to Manchester City within hours of the transfer window opening. Michael Owen's agents have sent a brochure extolling his virtues to interested parties, including the Villa. Newcastle haven't managed to find a loophole that says they can stay in the Premier League after all. Lee Hendrie got sent off at Wembley in the play-off finals. And Karren Brady stated on television that nobody's ever called her a bitch.

The heat's obviously getting to some people.

Also available from Heroes Publishing

STAR-SPANGLED VILLANS
by STEVE PENNELL

Take an under-achieving football club with huge expectations. Replace the unpopular boss with a highly-regarded star-name manager, and the much-maligned chairman with a billionaire philanthropist. Add a touch of bounding optimism and some American-style marketing flair. Success is sure to follow? Not necessarily, as Steve Pennell shows in this amusing and incisive look at the 2006/07 season as seen through the eyes of an old-school supporter of a new-fangled club.

"There are many words to describe football supporters – fanatics, loyalists, diehards – but few truly understand what lies at the soul of their club. Steve Pennell is one of this small, endangered breed." – Richard Whitehead; The Times.

Price – £5.99
ISBN 0954388461 – EAN 9780954388461

Also available from Heroes Publishing

DEMOLITION DERBIES & OTHER DELIGHTS
a season in Aston
by STEPHEN WHITEHOUSE

Season 2007-08 sees Year Two of the Lerner Revolution and things are going well in the world of Aston Villa. There's money being spent on new players, entertaining football to enjoy and two local derbies that will be remembered for years to come. Players are becoming international regulars, which proves to be a mixed blessing, and the Holte Hotel has been renovated, even if getting in there on matchdays proves trickier than anticipated.

All of this comes under the perceptive, unashamedly biased, gaze of Stephen Whitehouse, who can't help wondering when things are going to start going wrong.
After all, this is the Villa we're talking about.

Price - £5.99

ISBN 0955970806 – EAN 9780955970801

HEROES PUBLISHING
PO Box 1703, Perry Barr, Birmingham, B42 1UZ
www.heroespublishing.com